SATURDAY

news at 0600 hrs. and 0700 hrs., and a 5-minute news
Relaxing music interspersed with sport, leisure, sh
do, motoring trips, etc., and at 0845 hrs. we schedul
g spot.

time: 1 hour 45 minutes

1730 - 1800 hrs.:

1800 hrs.:

1810 hrs.:

1900 - 2000 hrs.:

~~ch will have been~~ Records, and the final stag
within the I.B.A. prescribed upper limit, I ne

Needle time: 25 minutes

lletin (5 mins.)
Show
ing the following basic
lar order):- Where to dri
activities for Sundays,
out zoos, bear gardens,
ntly baez-ed towards relig

ervice
to have this kind of progr
admit OB difficulties and
oduction involving two "re
ill include occasional ins
y well known guests. OB'
blic meetings is possible

: Community Council
airs with listener particip
nto next show.

s.)
record show.

ow, records, cleaned up hu
inks with Canada, Australia
rom Glen Daly/Lex MacLean/A.
1200-1300, personality, pre
entertainment, interviewe
half an hour.

John McCaf
Ian Wood

rogramme repeat. See Mon.-F

HA HA HA)

Record show with resident
nclude interviews with people
dictions, pop the question, c
Davis

p Thirty. *Steve Jones*

(friday afternoon)

1800-1930	Gentle MOR Record Show. Features include travel, odd jobs, character intervi and Radio Clyde's Pick of the Week's People.
1930-2000	Arts Magazine. On a rota basis we would handle such subjects as - music (new, old, good, bad, folk, punk), Arts Maga and the Underground Press; Poetry readings and live whenever possible. We are in contact with jazz and music societies; touring groups entirely possible.
2000-2100	The Great Classics. Records, and interviews with distinguished guests, including Alex Gibson, Yehudi Menuhin, Anthony Hop Hans Keller etc. Hopefully a show based on the gr period in classic music will begin to encourage a exceptance of newer music.
2100-2200	News (5 mins.). Education Programme-repeat of part of the week nig programme, but without the phone-in follow up. W instead direct conflict between educators and the as the second portion of this show.
2200-2400	Record and Chat Show. MOR music, fare proportion of instrumentals, list queries replied to by our own equivalent of Evely
2345-2400	Sci/fi and Horror Stories. A new man-in-black with synthesised music and tit Gallacher & Lyle.
2400-0200	Jazz Record Show. A platform for opinion, whether it be musicians public. Regular guests stars would be offered t to reveal their normally untapped views. Possib implementing Clyde's own recording sessions for transmission.

One week Humphrey Burton.
2nd week Ian Turple. 3rd week : Arts Council
Woxwell Geo

acceptance

JIM WAUGH i/c

the phone-in follow up.
t between educators and the publ
of this show.

GILIOH. JACK McL

Like anglept extrne

tion of instrumentals, listeners
our own equivalent of Evelyn Home.

y + Clyde orgin - multi-ussum go%

ries "guests and friends"
h synthesised music and titles by

washau costine - maggie
quest solo wist.

on, whether it be musicians of th
sts stars would be offered this,
ally untapped views. Possibility
own recording sessions for spre

WAUGH i/c.

sts. Sessions. eta

MONTY   SPORT?

The afternoon programme will give u
ball, racing, etc., and the occasio
All this will be interspersed with
hoping to negotiate into our programme from any footb
into our programme from any footb
music content drops to nil, and i
results programme.

Needle time: 1 hour 30 minutes

Alex i/c.

CLIFF

rs.:   Quiz programme - format yet

News including sport.

Omnibus repeat of the week

THIN

hrs.:   Competition time. Record
which will have been runn
within the I.B.A. prescr

Needle time: 25 minutes

Premiere:
200 hrs.:   2-minute news at 200
osts from two show

Alex/
No food van yet

0900 - 1100 hrs.:   2-minute news headlines. A junior choice selection of
interspersed with features primarily of interest to ch
including the best of "children talking" previously tr
Monday to Friday at this time.

Needle time: 1 hour 10 minutes

AP

SUNDAY

0800-0930   News Bulletin (5 mins.)
Morning Show   Ken McLeag
(including the following basic components -
particular order):- Where to drive today, O
leisure activities for Sundays, gardening,
info. about zoos, bear gardens, etc. The mu
be slightly baez-ed towards religion and tra

0930-1000   Sunday Service
(-1015)   Inorder to have this kind of programme from
have to admit OB difficulties and opt for and
Studio production involving two "reps." with m
Reading will include occasional inserts or su
material by well known guests. OB's from ope
Ann and public meetings is possible and would

1000-1100   'Access' : Community Council
(-1015)   Local affairs with listener participation - po   Alex
overflow into next show.

1100-1130   News (4 mins.)
Personality record show.   Pu-lee.   Ya

1130-1430   (Don Cunning)
Big family show, records, cleaned up humour from
terracing, links with Canada, Australia, etc., r
of excerpt from Glen Daly/Lex MacLean/A.N. Other
Headlines at 1200-1300, personality, preferably
football, or entertainment, interviewes and choos
records for half an hour.

A Pollic   John McCalman} PA
tom Wood }

1430-1530   Old Glasgow programme repeat. See Mon.-Fri. 2200

1530-1600   Golden Oldies. (HA HA HA)
DJ.   Record show with resident part-ti
the area;   predictions, pop the question, dedicati
etc.   Craig Joyis

1600-1800   Radio Clyde Top Thi

NOT
QUITE
ALTOGETHER
NOW!

DE W
261
5.1 D
EKLY
MME G
CLYDE W
YOUR WEEKLY RADIO CLYDE
rid.
BER 20

A run down on Radio Clydes'

AM: 6.00, 6.30, 7.00, 7.30, 8.00, 8.30, 9.00, 10.00, 11.00.

PM: 12.00, 1.00, 2.00, 4.0, 5.30, 7.00, 10.0

monday

JUNE 4

6.03
Breakfast Show
Beat these Monday blues with Dave Marshall — he'll get you to work with a little help from the AA reports, Flightwatch, and weather forecasts. Morning thought this week is given by Rev. Alex Gunn.

9.05
The Dougie Donnelly Mid-Morning Show
Double D brightens your day with music, dedications, competitions, Recipe Time with Sheila Duffy, and Fred Paton's chat for the over sixties around 11.30.

12.05
Richard Park's Lunchtime Show

4.02
Homeward Bound
Presented by Bill Smith. The programme that gets you home safely with music, traffic news, and several super Smith-style surprises.

5.30
Newsdesk
Radio Clyde's early evening news round-up.

5.45
Clydewide Tonight
including What's On in and around Glasgow this evening, the Telephone Top Five, and Gig Guide.

7.03
Westminster Now.

7.05
Noticeboard
Fiona Ross introduces a weekly programme that deals with all aspects of education. If you'd like to

the only person in the programme, but we'll give him star billing anyway. Maybe he'll phone you and have a blether. Maybe he won't. You'll have to wait and see . . .

10.05
Authors
Alex Dickson's guest tonight is Peter Habeler, whose book " Everest: Impossible Victory " was published recently.

10.30
Westminster Now
A nightly round-up of the day's Parliamentary proceedings.

10.35
The Anderson Folio
Iain Anderson introduces a mixture of music, poetry and prose. There's a section of the programme for Gaelic listeners, too. Entries for the Literary Competition to PO Box 261, Glasgow, G2 7LB.

tues

6.03
Breakfast Show
A cuppa tea and Dave Marshall are all you need to start the day.

9.05
The Dougie Donnelly Mid-Morning Show
Prizes to be won in the quiz section, plus a chance to add to your culinary collection with another of Sheila Duffy's recipes.

12.05
Richard Park's Lunchtime Show
Super sounds from the Tartan 30 plus travel information and sport.

11.58
Time Out
Some thoughts at the end of the day from Rev. Keith Steven.

wed

6.03
eakfast Show

NOT QUITE ALTOGETHER NOW!

A PIONEER'S TALE OF RADIO CLYDE

Tony Currie

Neil Wilson Publishing

First published by
Neil Wilson Publishing Ltd
0/2 19 Netherton Avenue
GLASGOW
G13 1BQ

Tel: 0141 954 8007
Fax: 0560 150 4806
E: info@nwp.co.uk
W: www.nwp.co.uk

A catalogue record of this book is
available from the British Library.

ISBN: 978-1-906476-08-3

First published in October 2009

OTHER BOOKS BY TONY CURRIE:
A Concise History of British Television 1930–2000
The Radio Times Story

Designed by Mark Blackadder.

Printed by CPod, Trowbridge.

CONTENTS

ACKNOWLEDGEMENTS

Much as writing a book seems a mostly solitary occupation, this volume owes its existence to the support of others. For a start, Andy Park and Jimmy Gordon whose faith in me kick-started my career in broadcasting and thence this book.

There are many others to be properly thanked before we get down to the serious business of the story. My wife Karin whose skills as a sub-editor have stood me in good stead for almost every piece of my writing that's ever been published and whose encouragement kept this project alive for over 13 years. Publisher Neil Wilson, who has likewise been godfather of this folio during its somewhat lengthy gestation.

Former colleagues have come up with photographs, stories, tea and biscuits or simply encouragement: Dave and Barbara Marshall, Andy Park, Steve Jones, Alex Dickson, Fiona Ross, Sheila Duffy, Colin MacDonald and Tom Steele. Alison Sykora provided photographs of her late father Ken, Barbara McRitchie gave me much of the archive of her late husband, Jimmy Mack; Cliff Hanley Jnr kindly gave permission for the reproduction of his 'DNA Man' cartoon strips.

DAVE

261 ═══════════════════ RADIO CLYDE LTD.

From the Managing Director

Registered Office:
Ranken House, Blythswood Court,
Anderston Cross Centre, Glasgow G2 7LB.
Telephone: 041-204 2555.
Telex No. 779537
Telegraphic Address: RADCLYDE
Registered in Scotland No. 43876.

STAFF NEWS LETTER NO. 1

It is my intention to write a short news letter to all staff roughly once a quarter just to ensure that everyone is fully in the picture and to comment of some matters that need mentioning.

1. **Programmes:**

Radio Clyde is the most successful radio station in Britain within its coverage area, and one cannot do much better than that. The early teething troubles were eliminated remarkably quickly, and I am now broadly satisfied with virtually all of our output and proud of an increasing proportion of it. Our success underlines the need there has been for local radio for this area - a need which was unfulfilled until the I.B.A. decided that Glasgow would be one of the first centres for independent local radio. Clearly our programme format and the concept of balanced programming on one frequency has also proved successful, and last, but by no means least the hard work and creative talents of our staff have produced in many cases programmes which stand comparison with anything. There is a final factor which I would mention which, 'though the most important of all, is perhaps the most difficult to define and therefore impossible to achieve if it is not already there. I refer to a rapport with the audience. There are times when I feel that the bond between Radio Clyde and its listeners is almost tangible. This is all-important. Were we to patronise our audience, it would disappear over-night. For this very reason, it is extremely important that despite the inevitable pressures and frustrations of work we are always polite to any callers and willing wherever possible to undertake engagements, usually at no fee, for worthy causes in the area. This is time-consuming, but important if we are to retain the affection of our listeners.

2. **Audience Figures:**

As you are all no doubt aware, four separate surveys (plus, I suspect, the B.B.C.'s own audience research figures) all put Radio Clyde running ahead of any single B.B.C. station. This is nothing short of a broad-casting revolution - I doubt if there has ever been a station anywhere which, within six weeks of coming on air, had assumed a leading place in its own market. Again, congratulations to all concerned - which means the entire staff. For the record, the N.O.P. survey shows that about half the population listen to Radio Clyde at some point in each day, and over 70% listen at some point each week.

Directors: F. I. Chapman (Chairman), James Gordon (Managing Director), William Brown C.B.E., J. Dickson Mabon M.P., Kenneth McKellar, A. J. Murray C.A., Sir Iain Stewart, Esmond Wright.

FOREWORD

This book is not intended as a definitive history of Radio Clyde. Some day, perhaps, the official story will be told of how a group of like-minded people in the business of media got together in the North British Hotel in Glasgow on 20 April 1972 and set up what was to become the most successful local radio station in Britain.

Within these pages you will find the recollections and sometimes disjointed anecdotes of just one of the station's pioneers. Inevitably, my view of those early days was from the floor. In the giddy heights of the managing director's stratosphere the view would no doubt have been significantly different.

But this book isn't about the way in which the company was managed (although it has to be said that, for most of the time, it seemed to be managed particularly successfully), it is about the laughter and tears that those of us who helped to create the programmes shared each day. It is about scenes behind the things that those who tuned in to 261metres or 95.1MHz are most likely to remember. It's the story of a family. This is for everyone in our 'family' who made the early days of Radio Clyde the happiest of my life.

Tony Currie

... McLeod / Gill Martin, #6
#45

e-MOR Record Show
res include travel, odd jobs, ch
adio Clyde's Pick of the Week's

Magazine
rota basis we would handle suc
c (new, old, good, bad, folk, p
the Underground Press; Poetry r
ever possible. We are in conta
societies; touring groups e
week Humphrey Burton.

Omnibus repeat of THINGS

GLASGOW HERALD Friday April 6 1973   13

Radio Clyde Limited

Radio Clyde invites applications for some senior management positions. This is an entirely new field. We are looking for highly adaptable men and women of outstanding ability and with considerable initiative and enthusiasm. Conditions of service will include pension scheme and life assurance and the opportunity to participate in the shareholding of the company.

Sales Manager: £4500 plus

Media sales experience is essential. The person we seek should be accustomed to dealing at a senior level with advertising agencies.

Chief Accountant: £3500-£4000

The successful applicant should be a qualified accountant with previous experience in office management and credit control, preferably in the field of communications or entertainment. Experience of a computer installation would be an advantage. He will be required to install a system of budgetary control and to produce regular management accounts.

Chief Engineer: £3500-£4000

The person we seek must be experienced in controlling the operation and maintenance of audio equipment to I.B.A. standards.

The successful applicants will take up their position some months ...

Radio Clyde

BROADCASTERS

Knowledge of this area essential. Broadcasting experience preferable. There will be an intensive training period, at full salary, prior to the station going on the air.

News

Experience in radio or television broadcasting, newspapers or a proven interest in and knowledge of current affairs essential.
Apply to Head of News.

Entertainment

'Disc Jockeys' and General Station Presenters.
Apply to Head of Entertainment.

News Copy Typists/Secretaries

Fast speeds essential. Capable of working under pressure.
Apply to Head of News.

TECHNICIA

Operational and maintenanc in studio and on outside bro

Programme Se Co-ordinator

To assist in scheduling of pe studio facilities. Previous ex in broadcasting desirable.
Apply to Chief Engineer.

SITUATIONS VACANT

GLASGOW HERALD Wednesday July 4 1973

RADIO CLYDE

HEAD OF NEWS £4,500
HEAD OF ENTERTAINMENT £4,500-£5,000
CHIEF ACCOUNTANT £4,000 plus
CHIEF COPYWRITER £3,500

HEAD OF NEWS

He will be responsible for liaison with all important news sources and for ensuring adequate coverage of all events relevant to this area. He is responsible for all news and information broadcast by the station.

HEAD OF ENTERTAINMENT

Thorough knowledge of music both live and recorded is essential and a knowledge of drama would be desirable. He is responsible for daily scheduling of programmes.
Radio Clyde invites applications for the two senior management appointments in the broadcasting field. They will be responsible to the Managing Director for the implementation of Radio Clyde's programme plans as submitted to the I.B.A. and for the creation and execution of new programme ideas. Broadcasting experience and a knowledge of and feeling for Glasgow and the West of Scotland are essential.

CHIEF ACCOUNTANT

The successful applicant should be a qualified accountant with previous experience in office management and credit control, preferably in the field of broadcasting or advertising. He will be required to install a system of budgetary control and to produce regular management accounts.

CHIEF COPYWRITER

Responsible for the creation and writing of imaginative commercials where these are not supplied by the advertiser.
Conditions of service include pension scheme and life assurance, an opportunity to participate in the shareholding of the company.

Applicants should give full details of education, experience, and present salary and state the post for which they are applying.
All applications will be treated in strictest confidence and should be addressed to:

RADIO CLYDE
16 FITZROY PLACE
GLASGOW, G3 7RW

PENSIONS

5 minutes

Pop Party. Apart from 2-minute news headlines at 2200 hrs., 2400 hrs., at 0200 hrs., this is music all the way with a heavy

GETTING IT ALTOGETHER

11 October 1973

Ruby, the receptionist and switchboard operator was sitting on an upturned packing case, huddled in an overcoat when I first arrived on a drizzly autumn afternoon at what appeared to be a building site in the middle of Glasgow's gloomy Anderston Cross Centre. I had come for an interview for a presenter's job with Radio Clyde, due to go on the air at the end of the year.

'You're here to see Andy Park?' she quizzed.

I nodded. Out of dear knows how many thousands of demo tapes he'd been on the receiving end of, the station's Head of Entertainment had apparently been sufficiently impressed to grant me an interview. But as I was about to find out, only just.

Ushered into his temporary office, I noted one chair, one desk, several hundred reels of tape, and one small, dark, bearded man. His greeting was not altogether what I had expected.

'So what the fuck's this then, wee pal?' Andy Park was not a man to mince words.

'It's my demo tape.'

'It's only one minute long. Go away and do me a proper one and then I might listen to it.'

End of interview.

A few weeks and one 'proper' demo tape later – on 12 November 1973 – I resigned my job as manager of Talisman Hi-Fi and officially joined the team at Radio Clyde Ltd, Scotland's first licensed, land-based, commercial radio station. This was just a few days after photocopier salesman and longstanding chum from our hospital broadcasting days, Dave Marshall, had persuaded Andy Park of his dual need for a photocopier and a breakfast jock. The copier has long since been junked, but Dave Marshall has never faltered. Until he left Clyde for Saga Radio and thence Smooth, he was to become the longest-surviving breakfast show presenter in the entire world!

On day one I was introduced to some of the 261 crew already

Andy Park

1

Posing moodily in what was to become Studio B (left to right): Jimmy Gordon, Tom Steele, Andy Park, Sheila Duffy and Alex Dickson.

Alex Dickson's temporary office. Alex consults with Tom Steele and Sheila Duffy poses with one of the first batch of T-shirts. Note that she is not wearing it. Indeed she never did.

in place. Annie Wood – 'Producer, fixer, researcher, whatever' who had left the BBC for a spot of excitement. John MacCalman, another old friend from hospital radio – producer, presenter, technician, magician and general dogsbody (still freelancing as overnight presenter for the station, he has even more staying power than Dave Marshall). John appeared to benefit from the rare talent of apparently surviving for lengthy periods without the need for sleep.

Sheila Duffy, former STV news presenter was already something of a household name, and a lady whom I held in a certain awe … well, for almost a whole fortnight.

Margaret Jane Cockburn, sometime jazz singer with Humphrey Lyttleton; ex-rally driver; ex-dancer; ex-pianist and ex-'Voice of Kenya' broadcaster. Sandra Fraser, the no-nonsense lassie in charge of the record library. 'Now wee pal (everybody seemed to be 'wee pals' at 261) gie's a hand wi' these 200 boxes of LPs and I'll gie ye the new Johnny Harris album!'

I did.

She did.

And I treasure it to this day.

Then along came the 'Tiger'.

Tiger Tim Stevens (real name Jimmy McCrory) like John MacCalman, had worked for British Rail. But that was in another life. For his first assault on the Anderston Cross offices, he kicked open the brand new front doors, and – dressed in a fake fur tiger suit and brandishing a not very real-looking rifle – demanded to see 'the bossman'.

Ruby was – as was her custom – impressively nonplussed.

'Along the right hand corridor.'

'Aye. Right. Well, he'd better watch out.'

The Tiger stalked his prey. The first door he came to presumably had a promising sort of feel about it. He pushed it open.

It was the kitchenette.

He was confronted by the equally scary Sheila Duffy or 'Duffs' as she was known, a cultured lady from Edinburgh with all the sass of her Glasgow years at STV.

She was clutching an implausibly sized cup into which she was pouring a truly enormous quantity of tea.

She sized up the lad with the pop gun with some disdain. 'Oh. I say … '

A deflated Tiger scarpered sharpish.

He reappeared a few days later, wearing his best suit and being thoroughly polite to everyone. *Especially* Duffs.

He got the job, of course.

I became aware that there were apparently four different breeds within Glasgow's embryonic radio station. First and foremost (as far as I was concerned in those first few days) there was 'Park's Department' – Andy's brave band of entertainers. Second, the newsroom, presided over by the jovial and manic memo-writer Alex Dickson. His journalists, largely drawn from defunct sections of the Scottish press (eg the *Scottish Daily Mail* and the *Scottish Daily Express*, both of which had recently made most of their Glasgow staff redundant) seemed to live in perpetual fear of their bombastic and somewhat irascible boss. He would breeze in to the jocks' office, from time to time bellowing: 'Plenty more where you came from – shake 'em out the trees,' before drifting into his own office to compose the umpteenth challenging memo of the morning. Someone whose name I cannot mention even to this day for fear of awful reprisals *papered the newsroom walls* with Alex's memos. An awesome sight!

Then there were the engineers – all guys with but one exception – who generally seemed a good deal calmer unless acrid smoke was

Night or day, John MacCalman was never off duty!

The Tiger

emanating from one of their shiny new toys. Led by the amiable and able John Lawrie Lumsden, who had already been chief engineer of the floating pirate Radio Scotland, they would bustle around wielding soldering irons, screwdrivers and splicing tape. For them the business of building new studios from scratch was evidently the very best bit.

And there was the sales department, essential to any commercial radio operation, yet curiously shunned by the programme makers. Peter Elliot was the man in charge, and it reinforces their invisible image that – decades later – I can only recall two of them. A rather highly strung lady named Anne Budge (poor soul, she had no chance of escaping the nickname 'budgie') and a lively and diminutive (ie even shorter than me) bloke by the name of Neil Dunn. Were they the stars of sales, perhaps?

These four groups, it seemed, worked on totally different planets – yet in the end all four proved equally necessary for the station's survival.

The period leading up to the opening night – Hogmanay, 1973 – was, and remains to this day, a blur. But there are bits that have stuck in the memory. Like the morning Tom Steele (Dickson's number two) and I were dispatched to purchase a camp bed and a sleeping bag. Both of us considered this an ominous portent. Soon I was to find myself a regular occupant of the selfsame bed and bag as recording and preparation sessions continued well into each night, and a well-timed rail strike put the kybosh on me going home to Ardrossan on the Ayrshire coast.

I moved to a flat in Glasgow, near to the studios. But I *still* found myself sleeping in the building as the on-air deadline drew ever nearer. There was just so much to be done – and so little time left to fit it all in. Each DJ had their own set of jingles, and that meant copying every individual jingle a dozen or so times on to individual tape cartridges, a dull and labour-intensive process.

Ah, cartridges. These took pride of place in the radio firmament. Little blue plastic packs containing continuous loops of tape, playing anything from 20 seconds to ten-and-a-half minutes and designed to make it simple to play short items like commercials, jingles and news reports. But they were far from perfect. For a start, the recording machine didn't wipe the tape (unlike cassette recorders) so each 'cart' had to be hand-erased in a terrifying instrument known as a 'bulk eraser'. This large and unfeasibly heavy wooden box had a front slot a bit like a letterbox, and when a tape was inserted a heavy magnetic field would be created, wiping

the original recording. The bulk eraser could also ruin your watch if you forgot to take it off first.

It was also possible to remove a 'cart' that had been played from the machine before it had found its way back to the beginning of the loop, which meant the next time the 'cart' was played, listeners were treated to the deadly 'whoosh-whoosh' sound of bulk-erased tape instead of the intended item.

These little packs could also become mechanically unstable, and could seriously mangle their contents, usually at the most inopportune moments. Nowadays they have been replaced by hard disk playout systems that are slightly more reliable. More of 'carts' later …

Alex Dickson, Tom Steele and I spent an all-night session choosing theme tunes for all the news programmes. With my anorak's knowledge of the specialist music libraries that provided records for radio and TV use only, I must have played them hundreds of suggested tracks that night as we decided on the introductory music for programmes like 'Clyde Comment', 'News Special', 'Plain Man's Guide', and many others; all naturally requiring multiple copies on more of the ubiquitous 'carts' of course …

An excited buzz went around the jocks' office one Monday that Clyde had hired a 'star name' from BBC Radio 1. He would be joining us to host the prestigious mid-morning show. Speculation was naturally rife, and when it turned out to be Steve Jones, there was simultaneous disappointment and some relief that we weren't going to have to try to compete with the likes of 'Fluff' Freeman or Tony Blackburn!

An early staff photo, left to right: Gerry Bain, John Lumsden, Tom Steele, Paul Murricane, a news secretary whose name I can't remember, Jimmy Gordon, Bob King, Christine Brisbane, George Mackintosh, George Montgomery, Craig Samet, Richard Roy, Alex Dickson, Ruby Macgregor, Elisabeth Simpson and Judith Landless.

Pre-Clyde, Steve Jones (left) visiting Glasgow to host a Radio 1 Club. The producer on his right is Ben Lyons who for many years was BBC Scotland's most energetic and successful radio producer.

When the Jones Boy arrived in person a few days later at the end of November, he turned out to be urbane, charming, witty, thoroughly professional – and a lifelong friend.

The rest of the broadcasting family quickly occupied the few remaining empty desks in the jocks' office. Richard Park from Kirkcaldy, an ex-pirate who had also worked for Radio 1, was put in charge of lunchtime. Ben Harris, a tall man who was a little older than the rest of us, was introduced to us as Maggie's co-host on the 'Afternoon Show'.

Teenager Ken Page, yet another of our gang from hospital radio days, was detailed to compile the daily childrens' quarter of an hour. *Scottish Daily Express* man Colin MacDonald was handed a 15-minute comedy slot every afternoon as well as one of the midnight shows. Some familiar faces from STV turned up to fill freelance slots.

The press began to take an interest. Even in my home town, a *Scottish Daily Express* billboard was plonked outside my local newsagent with the words 'Ardrossan DJ set for stardom.' My Dad shelled out for a dozen copies and the billboard as well! But I have always suspected that dozens of other similar billboards appeared across Scotland on the same day ... in the article inside the paper, *Express* man James Taylor wrote, 'his polished voice could well earn him a fortune.' Aye, right. I'm still waiting!

In the blur of memory so many decades later, I can vividly recall the outstanding moment when all the DJs assembled one morning in Studio B as Andy Park threaded up one of the most important reels of tape in the building. The first playing of the Radio Clyde jingles.

One of the crucial elements in any radio station's lexicon of sound is its jingles. At this point in the 21st century, the fashion is for a single voice announcing the station name over electronic whooshes and zaps. They're called 'sweepers'. But in 1973, the height of wireless fashion was a set of catchy little musical items with the station name sung in multi-part harmony. This style had originated in the US city of Dallas in 1951, and by the 70s almost every US station had its call letters sung in harmony ten times in every show. Practically every jingle emanated from one of the big production houses in Dallas – PAMS, Pepper-Tanner, Gwinsound or TM Productions.

Radio Clyde had cleverly opted for something different, though. The outstanding jingles were crafted by Canadian Dolores Claman and her husband Richard Morris for the comparatively unknown British company, Emison, owned by the giant EMI Records. Claman was already a very successful composer in her home country, having written the striking 'A Place to Stand' for the 1967 Expo and the enduring TV ice-hockey theme that many still consider to be Canada's 'second national anthem'.

Colin MacDonald

She used her skills to the full on the Emison package together with the vocals of well-known Scottish singers Danny Street and Margaret Savage (who had enjoyed TV fame with the 'Black & White Minstrel Show'). With the catchy tags 'altogether happy', 'altogether guys' and of course the uniquely Glaswegian 'altogether stoatin'' they instantly caught the imagination of our punters. Once Clyde was on the air, we'd be followed about by kids bellowing 'Radio Clyde two-six-wan!' wherever we went.

That first hearing was pure magic. We all stood in silence with silly big grins on our faces when we realised how stylishly we were going to brighten up our shows with these little gems of aural excitement. This was going to be good! As the air date drew ever nearer, Anderston Cross became a 24-hour-a-day blur of even more intense activity and excitement as plans for all those new shows and new ways of broadcasting started to gel. We'd set five precedents every morning before breakfast!

The main DJ studios weren't ready at the beginning of December, so to begin with the vast electronic gubbins that makes it all work – presentation mixer, turntables and spot cartridge players – were dumped on a wee table in the middle of the large music-recording Studio B so that we could start playing with them. It all resembled the flight deck of a 747, and none of us was going to have a co-pilot! But John Lumsden and his team had the main Studio A and the master control and news studios sufficiently ready for the start of test transmissions on 7 December. As Radio Clyde did not officially launch until 31 December, these tests were made by 'The Engineering Information Department of the Independent

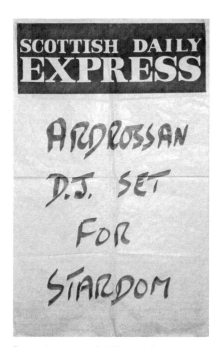

SCOTTISH DAILY EXPRESS

ARDROSSAN D.J. SET FOR STARDOM

Depends on your definition of stardom ...

Broadcasting Authority'. They were made up from two hour-long tapes with frequent long-winded and stiffly formal announcements recorded by Managing Director James Gordon (himself an ex-STV presenter), together with Maggie, Dave and me. They included a bizarre selection of music – everything from Mendelssohn's 'Fingal's Cave' to the Beatles' 'Lovely Rita', compiled by a young man with the unlikely name of Davy Crockett! Davy was, in fact, the chap from the IBA in charge of determining whether our studios were technically up to scratch, and we had to have a clean bill of health from him before we were permitted to go live. A frustrated radio producer, Davy had wangled himself the nice job of compiling test tapes – firstly those used in London before the start of its two commercial stations, LBC and Capital radio two months earlier and then for Clyde.

Our two reels were played continuously 24-hours-a-day from 9.30am on 7 December until the moment we opened, so within days everybody in the building – if not the west of Scotland – was able to recite Mr Crockett's musical selections by heart. Some may still be able to do so!

Being the very first stereo radio transmissions in Scotland, they caused quite a stir and I know that Davy chose much of the music to impress hi-fi buffs, as it surely did.

There were some glitches in the tests, however. Theoretically, the daytime (9am to 7pm) was transmitted in stereo from tape machines in Radio Clyde's master control room under the watchful eye of John Lumsden. Then in the evening, the control room at the IBA's transmitter at Black Hill near Shotts would take over, playing the tapes in mono from the same machines that had been used during the daytime for ITV's testcard music.

But sometimes the boys at Black Hill would forget about this added routine, and the airwaves would resound to the sound of silence for an hour or two. Worse, because of a switching error, the casual antics of one of the DJs who was having a quiet practice after-hours in Studio A, were broadcast live, nearly causing Davy Crockett to crash his car in his panic-stricken haste to get back to the studios and warn the innocent presenter that his professional debut had come unexpectedly early.

Although still some way off being ready, the studios were officially opened by Lord Aylestone, the chairman of the IBA, on Friday 14 December.

We all wore our best frocks and suits (my *only* suit) and the offices were crammed with VIPs as we did our best to convince the

assembled gathering of our competence to be in charge of a broadcasting station.

Doubtless poured by members of Andy Park's department, the
drink flowed freely, (particularly in the direction of the advertising
sales team. Ahem). The fun of socialising with the 'high heid yins'
was rather spoiled by having to thumb a lift back home after
missing the last bus! Next day it was back to T-shirts and
paperwork. We all had to learn the art of completing endless forms.
For every second of every record played, it was apparently necessary
to complete – in triplicate – what we called a 'P as B'. This stands
for 'programme as broadcast' on which we had to write the names
of each performer, song title, composer, publisher, record label,
catalogue number and duration.

These could take ages of tedium to complete, so we devised
shortcuts, frequently *guessing* the durations rather than playing the
record all the way through and timing it
with a stopwatch.

'How long's 'Love me Do' TC?'

'Oh – call it two minutes forty!'

With just a fortnight to go, the
'dry runs' started – a more or less full
service but we didn't send it 'down the
line' to the transmitters. Instead our
'listeners' were Messrs Gordon, Park,
and Dickson who formed a highly
critical trio, hanging on our every
word.

A cautious invitation from the MD.

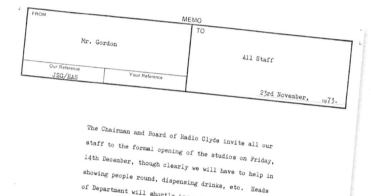

The official party in
the unfinished Studio A
for the grand opening,
(left to right): Kenneth
McKellar, Jimmy
Gordon, Ian Chapman,
Lord Aylestone
(seated) and John
Lumsden.

As Hogmanay got closer, we teased listeners who were enduring our test transmissions by 'leaking' ten minutes or so of these dry runs every few hours out live to the transmitters so that snatches of our tests could be heard outside in the real world, and hopefully whet the appetites of our pioneer west of Scotland listeners for the real thing.

The very first such 'leak' was part of my teatime show 'Homeward Bound' and the thrill of switching my headphones from 'Desk' to 'Off Air' and hearing my voice coming back at me from a radio receiver for the very first time is unforgettable.

The first real programme for transmission that we ever made in Studio A was Frank Skerret's 'When Music Was Music' recorded three days before Christmas. The studio door hadn't even been fitted so Andy Park stood guard to repel unwanted visitors while I sat at the control desk and put on the records for Frank – a task which I continued to undertake for him until the day I left Radio Clyde. Oddly, I don't recall ever hearing Frank refer to the show by its published title, which I think was dreamed up by Andy Park.

For Christmas Day 1973, I had the honour of producing a special two-hour test transmission tape. Davy Crockett had returned to London, and the IBA – uniquely – had agreed to let us 'do our own thing'. On Christmas Eve I had the time of my life compiling two hours of all sorts of Christmas music, from the Black and White Minstrels to Herb Alpert and the Tijuana Brass. Waking up on Christmas morning to hear 'my tape' coming out of my own tranny at home was better than anything in that year's Christmas stocking! None of us was permitted more than 48 hours' celebrations (it felt like shore leave) before it was back to the studios as the nerve-wracking countdown to on-air began in earnest.

Three days to go, and the *Evening Citizen*, in an 'exclusive' interview with Jimmy Gordon, 'revealed' that no decision had been made concerning the host of the all-important opening show. Jimmy said: 'We haven't decided who will do the first broadcast, even. Probably the person who is scheduled for that day.' On that

Just one of the forms we had to fill in ...

basis it should have been the velvet-voiced Iain Anderson with his eclectic 'Anderson Folio'.

I have no recollection of the moment Andy Park told me that I'd been chosen for the gig. Apart from recalling that beforehand I stuck to drinking water as if my life depended on it, I remember nothing of what happened until about ten o'clock that evening when the mists of time suddenly cleared. An unreal stillness fell over Studio A. Andy Park and I sat alone, saying little to each other. The clock ticked. The mixing desk was silent, the needles in the various meters still. Unsettling.

10.28pm.

I pressed a button on the 'Spotmaster' cartridge machine, and from within the blue plastic pack of tape came the recorded voices of our jingle singers.

'Radio Clyde ... two six one ... we're Altogether Now!'

The Boss. Jimmy Gordon.

Another 'cart'. This one contained 60-seconds' worth of the voice of the Rev Andrew Herron, Moderator of the General Assembly of the Church of Scotland, wittering on predictably about ships and blessing all those who were to 'sail in the good ship Radio Clyde'. Did he think we were pirates?

At last it was my turn. Live. The first voice not to be prepackaged in plastic. I announced that the news would now be read by Paul Murricane.

I had practised his name all day, remembering that it rhymes with 'hurricane'. But my brain must have turned to jelly because I heard myself pronouncing the word 'Mew-rick-cane'. Damn!

Paul was seated in the little news studio (more of a glass-walled cupboard, really) to my left. He had been there for quite some time. He looked ... well, apprehensive. I pressed the button to start the jolly news jingle, faded up his microphone and cued him to begin the station's very first news bulletin.

He spoke.

I couldn't hear him.

Neither could anybody at home.

Panic!

John Lumsden, sitting at the master control panel through the glass, turned slightly ashen. Paul's lips continued to mouth the horribly silent bulletin. The jingle (a repetitive instrumental that sounded suspiciously like Jerome Moross's theme for 'The Big Country') finally ran out. Andy looked accusingly in my direction. A dozen hitherto disinterested newspaper reporters blocking the corridor through to the news studio were suddenly paying attention

DID WE SAY THAT?

When Clyde launched, the press were eager to speak to us, but less so to actually write down what we said. Some of the quotes attributed to us were truly laughable.

The *Scottish Daily Express* tipped me as 'the station's star DJ'. (On that basis I certainly wouldn't have paid much heed to Peter O'Sullivan's racing tips). They quoted me as saying, 'I've no particular market in mind. I like all classics, pop, folk and all facets of music, and I like chatting up people on the blower.' The blower?

Dave Marshall is reputed to have said, 'I don't want to be all airs and graces. I hate fancy accents.' What he certainly did say was, 'My previous employers were not too disappointed when I told then I was leaving. After all they ended up with the contract for supplying the station's duplicators!'

Andy Park: 'The opportunity to promote musical and dramatic talent on Radio Clyde is immense. I will be travelling thousands of miles in my quest for all kinds of entertainers suitable for radio. I am just as likely to pop into an amateur production in a village hall, as into the professional areas of music and drama.'

Jimmy Gordon: 'About half the programme will be records. The rest will largely consist of a look at the world through west of Scotland eyes ... we hope that the station will allow an upsurge of local talent and it will be basically a west of Scotland show.'

Jimmy again: 'If one of the announcers faints I could always stand in. In fact there are quite a few in this building who could stand in.'

Maggie Cockburn: 'Once we're on the air I hope to get a local ballooning club going.'

Robyn Herrick, Evening Citizen, 28 December 1973: 'When Radio Clyde decided 10.30pm on Hogmanay was the right time to flick the switch that will launch Scotland's first commercial radio station, they received a frantic call from London. It came from an advertising agency who asked the question: "Won't your listeners be too drunk to tune in?" The reply from Radio Clyde's managing director, Jimmy Gordon, was short. "That's not the question. The question is - won't they be too drunk to turn it off?" he said.'

Music Week: 'Greek-born Steve Jones ... ' He was born in Crewe. As Fiona Ross would say - 'mince!!'

to the goings-on behind the glass.

I threw open the fader for my own microphone again.

' ... er ... the best laid schemes of mice and ... um ... '

My microphone no longer worked, either. Instead I heard myself as if incarcerated in a public convenience being picked up – just – by another microphone on the other side of the room.

An inner voice. Don't panic now, Tony. It's only radio. Not brain surgery. Nobody dies if you make a mistake. Try this button.

This time I could hear myself properly.

'Best laid schemes of mice and men – Paul Murricane can't be found ... well, you have to have a bit of fun at the beginning, just to keep the adrenaline going! Paul – come through and read the news from here.'

As I slowly intoned the station's frequencies, Paul elbowed his way gingerly through the crowd of onlookers, pressmen, VIPs and hangers-on, charging like a bull into Studio A, hurling himself into the chair and ...

' ... Paul's here with the news. Paul – it's all yours.'

Radio Clyde was on the air.

ROOTS IN SCOTLAND AND AT SEA

'Outlook for Clyde is set Fair' was typical of the press headlines in the days following our launch. Broadcasting history in Scotland was made with Radio Clyde's opening transmission.

The forebears of Scotland's first commercial station go back to 1922. Scottish broadcasting began at 141 Bath Street, Glasgow where a Mr JMA Cameron ran his experimental ten-watt transmitter (Clyde's medium wave transmitter puts out 2,000 watts), with the callsign 5MG. On 6 March the following year, the British Broadcasting Company – a brand new commercial company formed by a consortium of wireless manufacturers – established the first full-scale daily broadcasting station a few doors away at 202 Bath Street.[1]

Mr Cameron was appointed 'The Engineer.' For a time he was the BBC's one and only engineer, the transmitter and control room being run by technical folk belonging to the installing companies. Herbert Carruthers was named as the Station Director, with a staff of three to help him run Scotland's first broadcasting station, 5SC. These were Alex Paterson, Mungo M Dewar and Kathleen Garscadden ('Auntie Kathleen') who remained with BBC Scotland for her entire working life. Her 'We Want to Broadcast' programme was responsible for introducing many of the country's best known broadcasters to radio whilst still in their teens.

The studio at 202 Bath Street was about 30-square feet and draped with grey hessian. It must have felt like the Black Hole of Calcutta when a full-sized orchestra was playing!

The Glasgow BBC station produced most of its own programmes initially, but as technology improved, it became possible to use telephone lines to bring programmes to the Scottish transmitter from stations in London, Manchester, Birmingham and further afield. And the BBC – ruled like a rod of iron by the idiosy- cratic Stonehaven-born John Reith – quickly put all its provincial

---

1 It wasn't until 1927 that the BBC received its Royal Charter and became a Corporation.

Technology moved just as fast in the 1920s. A mere 12 months separates these photographs of the 5SC Control Room in Bath Street. The first (above) was taken in 1923, the second (right) a year later.

Scotland's radio pioneers including Alex Paterson (on drums), Mungo M Dewar (at the piano) and Auntie Kathleen conducting the 'Radio Circle' band in the BBC's 202 Bath Street studio in 1924.

stations, including the Scottish ones, under increasing pressure to take the 'quality' programmes from London rather than produce their own 'inferior' versions ...

Aberdeen acquired its own station on 10 October 1923, but Edinburgh and Dundee were confined to 'relay' status (producing fewer of their own programmes and using low-power transmitters) when they opened on 1 May and 12 November 1924 respectively.

As the demand for more and more radio grew, listeners put pressure on the BBC to provide an 'alternative' programme. As

there was a scarcity of suitable frequencies and technical restraints on the transmitter power, the company abandoned its string of 'local' stations and provided instead two nationally available services, one of which had a number of Scottish-originated programmes inserted into it from studios in Glasgow, Edinburgh and Aberdeen.

Thus on 25 September 1933, most of Scotland found itself with a choice between the BBC National Programme (ironically transmitted on 261 metres, medium wave!) and the BBC Scottish Regional Programme, both transmitted from the brand-new station at Westerglen, near Falkirk with its landmark high masts.

The 'Scottish Programme' offered around three hours a day (out of a total of thirteen-and-three-quarters) of Scottish material, with the rest coming chiefly from that centre of excellence – London. Come the war and what the BBC irritatingly referred to as 'regional broadcasting' was suspended on 1 September 1939, replaced by a common Home Service programme serving the whole of the UK. Scotland's share on an average 17-hour-day was often little over an hour-and-a-half.

When the war ended in 1945 the BBC restored 'regional' service, now christened the Scottish Home Service. At the start it continued to be an hour to an hour-and-a-half each day originated in Scotland; by 1965 the Scottish Home Service was broadcasting anything from two to five hours each day of purely Scottish programmes.

But the broadcasting firmament in Scotland was about to be shaken. At ten minutes to midnight on Hogmanay 1965, radio sets tuned to 242 metres in the medium waveband produced a whole new sound. A piper played 'The Black Bear' (ironically in an arrangement by Englishman Malcolm Arnold), and prominent Scottish broadcaster (and ex-BBC man) David Kinnaird led the countdown to 'the bells'.

'Scotland's Sound Sensation' – the newest of Britain's ever-growing fleet of pirate radio ships – Radio Scotland – was born, and the *News of the World* and Jean Macgregor Soups became the first advertisers on Scotland's new medium. The station was the brainchild of Glaswegian Thomas Victor Shields (known to all as 'Tommy') an ex-newspaper reporter turned publicity manager for STV. Whilst preparing a biography of Channel Ten's owner, Lord Thomson of Fleet, he had discovered that the foundation stone of that great man's media empire had been a commercial radio station. With his considerable knowledge of Scotland's media, Tommy

One of the giant BBC transmitting masts at Westerglen.

Pirate King - Tommy Shields.

Paul Young appears to be thinking about fish.

resolved to launch Scotland's first commercial radio station.

It wasn't easy finding a suitable boat. Once he followed a promising lead to a southern English harbour, but on pronouncing the name of the ship he had come to see, the harbourmaster handed him a lawyer's writ claiming thousands of pounds.

'Oh, I'm not the owner,' said Tommy quickly, 'just someone interested in looking at it.'

'Well,' said the harbourmaster, 'take a peek out of that window.'

All that was to be seen was the top of a mast sticking out of the water. The ship had sunk, and the writ was a claim against the owners for the cost of removing it from blocking the dock!

Eventually, Tommy found a 500-ton Clyde-built lightship, the *Comet,* in Ireland, and set about transforming it into a modern floating radio station. He anchored it in the Firth of Forth, four miles off Dunbar. The first DJ was young actor Paul Young (who was to marry Sheila Duffy and began his international fishing career as Clyde's 'fishing correspondent'). Paul had already achieved fame as a child star in the Bill Travers' film 'Geordie' and as co-presenter of 'Roundup' – STV's answer to 'Blue Peter', the same programme where Clyde boss Jimmy Gordon made his TV debut as quizmaster on a weekly schools' quiz segment.

Paul later dubbed the pirate ship 'a floating tip'. Tommy Shields described the conditions on board to prospective DJs as 'the last word in luxury'.

Jack McLaughlin recalls his first sight of the *Comet* as 'the biggest disappointment in my life. It was a rusty hulk with virtually no heating. Any heat you got came from a coal fire – and the coal was stored at the front of the boat. I spent my first night on board wrapped in a carpet to keep the cold out!' That was probably preferable to visiting the toilet, which as a result of arcing from the transmitter, had a habit of dispensing electric shocks to the under-sides of those who came into contact with it – according to Clyde's chief engineer John Lumsden who had held the same position with 261's pirate antecedent.

Also heard on '242' in its first months was 'The One O'Clock Gang'. This was based on the daily entertainment show that had

The Radio Scotland lightship - the *Comet.*

appeared on STV screens from its beginnings in 1957. Despite big audiences, Francis Essex, a new programme controller at STV (from down south), had decided to abandon lunchtime programmes a year earlier. Larry Marshall, Moira Briody and Tommy Maxwell recreated on Scotland's new radio the same magic that had attracted viewers each lunchtime for eight years.

Like other specially produced shows – 'Milligan's Mixture' (with STV chef Eric Milligan), 'Knockabout Pop' (Scotland's indigenous 'Juke Box Jury' presided over by Stuart Henry whose seasickness prevented him from working on board the *Comet*), 'Mallan's Medics' (with Peter Mallan who was also to join the Anderston Cross team a few years later) and 'Good Neighbours' (Tommy's own weekly charity spot) – 'The Gang' was produced at land-based studios in 'Radio Scotland House', a converted villa in Glasgow's Cranworth Street, a stone's throw from the rather larger BBC headquarters in Queen Margaret Drive.

Jimmy Mack – another of the station's early stars who eventually joined Radio Clyde – was unimpressed by the headquarters, as he told me years later. 'I often wondered if the house would sink before the ship did. If you go there today, there's just a big hole that's been turned into a sunken garden. Maybe if you dig down you'll find the roof buried underneath!'

Although he couldn't have realised it at the time, Tommy Shields had developed a unique programme format that appealed to all age groups and social classes. Unlike English pirates like Radio Caroline and Wonderful Radio London – that mostly based their programme formats on combinations of new releases and the current top 30 – '242' set out from the start to provide a complete programme service on one wavelength. It was the same format that was to make Clyde such a success nine years later.

Meanwhile, from the single cramped little studio on board the *Comet* – which former record-spinner Tony Allan described as 'slightly larger than a phone box' – the daily pop programmes 'Rooster Call', 'Now Hear This', 'Swing Across Midday' (or as Jack McLaughlin called it, 'Swing Across the Midden'), 'Laze Around', 'All Systems Go', 'Sophisticat' and 'Destination Midnight' were hosted in turn by the small crew of disc jockeys, each initially paid the princely sum of £20 a week for the privilege with food, board and coal included.

Although an instant success in the east, a poor signal in the west meant many found it hard to tune in, notably the influential advertising agencies based in Glasgow, so the ship was moved on 23 June

The crude, but effective home-built studio on board the *Comet*.

Jimmy Mack in his watery wireless days on board the *Comet*.

1966. With no on-board engines (lightships being built to house power-generating equipment for the lamp rather than for automotive power) it had to be towed by tug around the northern and western coasts to a new mooring in the Firth of Clyde, remaining on the air for the entire journey.

'When we arrived at Troon we switched off the transmitters for adjustments', remembers Jack McLaughlin. 'Somebody rowed out from a pub in Arran and we all piled into the boat and went across for a couple of drinks. That's what pirate radio was all about!'

At the end of July 1966, Harold Wilson's Labour Government threatened to make the pirates illegal on the grounds that they used unauthorised wavelengths, interfered with emergency radio communications and generally flouted the law.

The response of the pirates was to whip up as much support from their listeners as was humanly possible. Through its monthly glossy magazine '242', boss Tommy Shields made frequent and eloquent exhortations for Scotland to be exempt from the forthcoming legislation on the grounds that in some parts of the country, his was the only station that could be tuned-in satisfactorily. He offered to hand over his station to the government if they would promise to keep it on the air (they ignored the offer) and Shields stood as an independent candidate in the Pollok by-election, to no avail. A petition reputedly gathered two-and-a-half-million signatures, and a song was recorded with the chorus 'beat the ban and join the Clan on station '242'.'

In March 1967, Radio Scotland was forced off the air after being fined £80 for broadcasting illegally within territorial limits. Tommy Shields made the decision to close his station for good at midnight on 14 August, after further attempts to continue broadcasting from anchorages off Belfast and Fife Ness. A new Marine Offences Bill, outlawing radio pirates, received Royal Assent on 15 August. Tommy bade listeners farewell, declaring: 'This is the saddest hour of my life for this is the end of Radio Scotland. I shall shortly see a dream vanish before my eyes.'

In the end the company suffered a £100,000 loss and Tommy was heartbroken. He died from a kidney complaint within six months at the young age of 47. There are those who maintain the real cause was a broken heart.

But Tommy Shields' legacy to us all was that blueprint for Scotland's independent radio. Radio Clyde owes him much, and in recognition Richard Park presented a memorial to 242 on the seventh anniversary of the station's demise. With many of the

Richard Park was one of the youngest DJs on the pirate ships.

original '242' team live in the Anderston Cross studio it was appropriate that '261' should pay homage to its predecessor.

After the pirates had been wiped off the air, the government put pressure on the BBC to rethink its programming policies. A few months later in September 1967 they launched Radio 1 – complete with a team of ex-pirate DJs – and renamed their Light, Third and Home Services, as Radios 2, 3 and 4 respectively.

When the Wilson government was replaced by Ted Heath's Tories on 19 June 1970 they recognised the huge following the pirates had gained and set about creating a structure for legalised local commercial radio. They published a White Paper in March the following year outlining their plans for 60 new commercial stations throughout the UK.

As with all things parliamentary, it took another two years before the new Sound Broadcasting Act came into force on 12 July 1972, transforming the Independent Television Authority (under whose regulatory auspices ITV had been created) into the Independent Broadcasting Authority. The new IBA established a radio division, and issued advertisements inviting interested groups to apply for the franchises to operate the first batch of the new stations in September.

Glasgow was one of the first to be offered, with a catchment area of some 1.9 million potential listeners. On the closing date – 8 December 1972, there were four companies including Radio Glasgow Ltd and Radio Clyde Ltd applying for the contract. The IBA as always pondered the relative merits of the various consortia at length, and after holding public meetings and due deliberation, announced the award of a licence to Radio Clyde Ltd in March 1973.

The authority rented out to Radio Clyde the transmitter installations at Black Hill (for the 95.1 FM frequency) and Dechmont Hill (for 261m) for around £100,000 a year.

ON THE AIR

After the business with Paul's problem microphone, the three-and-a-half hours of 'Happy New 261' that followed were somewhat less stressful. Mixed in with the records were studio guests (many of them colleagues popping in to 'plug' their own shows), taped messages of good luck, including an interview I'd recorded a few days earlier with Kenneth McKellar who was a director of the station; messages from Jackie Stewart and Sean Connery, and a live outside broadcast at midnight to bring 'the bells' from the Tron into living room parties across the west of Scotland.

We also linked up with speech station, the London Broadcasting Company, whose launch I'd excitedly attended on 8 October. The original plan was to network half-an-hour of our programme to them, but in fact they plugged in to rather more than that, allowing Radio Clyde a substantial audience in the English capital that night.

Irritatingly, LBC's presenter, Dennis Rookard (by coincidence yet another old chum from hospital radio days) was intent on doing the 'phoney Scotsman' bit, complete with references to 'a braw bricht moonlicht nicht'. He even had a piper in the studio. But on Hogmanay we were all in forgiving mood.

LBC's Dennis Rookard is still broadcasting in 2009.

Then of course there were the commercials. Unlike those pirate ships and Radio Luxembourg, we worked under a legal requirement that these had to be carefully separated from the programme in such a way that there could be no doubt in the listener's mind that they were listening to a commercial break. This rule was policed by the IBA who went as far as to prohibit a presenter from voicing commercials within his or her own programme – a regular practice almost everywhere else in the world, and one which died out here eventually.

We were a teensy bit paranoid about not breaking these rules and losing our licence on the first night, so Andy decided that not only should we go into and out of commercial breaks with a short jingle, but we should separate each *individual* commercial with a jingle as well. The result was what nowadays would be referred to in radio circles as 'clutter'.

The first commercial break carried a recruitment advertisement for Strathclyde Police. It was a 60-second spot, with a voiceover that not only used an obviously phoney Scottish accent, but was also unable to pronounce Glasgow correctly! It was followed by an ad for the *Scottish Daily Express*, with Stanley Baxter providing all the character voices exquisitely. Subsequent breaks were a babble of jingles and advertisements. Of course, since listeners had never heard any of our little jingles before and didn't know their purpose, the result was total confusion, especially since in my eagerness to avoid 'dead air' (ie silence) several times I started the jingles before the commercials had actually finished. (This mercifully led to the universal practice of scribbling the final words on the label). After the third commercial break the practice was abandoned for good!

Radio Clyde's second news bulletin – at 11pm – was read by Craig Samet, who had come to 261 from one of the major American networks, giving him an apparent edge over his fellow reporters. Until his first bulletin, that was. He managed to mispronounce Lanarkshire, putting the emphasis on the 'ark' rather than the 'Lan'. Our switchboard lit up! 'Don't you people know how to pronounce the county you're in?' One newspaper reporter a few days later wrote, ' … some of the news team leave a great deal to be desired. The service is there, but the presentation, in many cases, has been somewhat poor. I won't embarrass the guy from Chicago by naming him, but dear, oh dear!'

When the first programme ended, Steve Jones and Richard Park took over at 2am for an all-night party. The station's phone lines were still jammed with listeners, mostly calling to wish us good luck. Ruby having gone home – well, she had to sometimes – it turned out, as luck would have it, that the only other person in the entire building who knew how to operate a PABX switchboard was yours truly!

Thus I found myself manning the phones all through the night until Ruby returned at eight the following morning. Most callers were complimentary; some listening far away from Glasgow, excited to have picked up our signals in places like Aberdeen and Brighton. Being Hogmanay, a few had unsurprisingly taken a wee refreshment. One demanded to know 'who was that English

Dave Marshall in Studio A in January 1974.

bastard who presented the first programme?' With some pride I gently explained that not only was I one hundred per cent Scottish, but that my parentage could be proved as well.

Daylight came, Ruby returned to her hot switchboard, and I was released to drift off home in a state of exhaustion and exhilaration. They might have let me have a wee dram or two before I left – but to be honest I can't recall ...

Clyde's first programme schedule was a hugely successful mix. Each weekday began at 6am with Clarkston-born Dave Marshall, one-time United Biscuits salesman with a passion for broadcasting. An original involvement with Glasgow's hospital radio setup led him and Norman Ross to be progenitors of Hospital Radio Paisley, and from the time I first met Dave in 1971 it had always been obvious that his future lay in radio. He'd taken a massive salary drop to come to Clyde – he was a successful photocopier salesman – but the risk proved worth taking. Such an attitude was not untypical – many folk would have paid just for the chance to work on Scotland's first land-based commercial station.

'Nine till Noon' belonged to tall, tanned and good-looking Steve – 'the Jones Boy'. Born in Crewe and with a variety of jobs behind him, at one time he was Lonnie Donegan's bass player and was even the vocalist on the 'B' side of one of Lonnie's singles. For some while before our launch he'd been the 'spare' jock at Radio 1. His wife, Lolita, joined him with the children later in the year once they'd found a suitable home in Glasgow. But in the early days, Steve lived out of a suitcase in a nearby hotel.

Lunchtime was the domain of Richard Park, aka 'Doctor Dick' (a name given to him by Steve Jones). Kirkcaldy-born Richard had to lie about his age in order to get his first job as a DJ on the pirate ship Radio Scotland. When '242' (as it was commonly known) was closed down by the government, Richard moved to Radio 1 to host roadshows from Scotland alongside Stuart Henry, before joining Clyde.

The afternoons were a bit of a problem. Andy's idea had been to team up Maggie Cockburn with Ben Harris for 'Two at Two'. But Ben took fright just a few days before we went on the air, and did a vanishing act. He telephoned from as far away as possible (Portsmouth, somebody said) to say that he'd made a ghastly mistake; that being a DJ just wasn't him; and that he was very sorry but wasn't coming back! Maggie was left to handle the show alone.

The Jones Boy on air in Studio A. Behind him is a stack of 'carts' containing commercials and sitting on that rack is 'Cabbie' a highland cow presented to us as a mascot by staff of the Cabin Bar next door.

This complicated little lady, with flowing locks and a colourful pedigree, lived alone with her collection of cats in a comfortable flat in Vinicombe Street, just off Byres Road in the West End. Maggie's life could never have been described as dull. Her problems were always larger than life. She fought incessantly with Andy Park, and had a different attitude from the rest of us, perhaps because she was a little bit older. (According to our press bumf Maggie was 31 in 1973, but most of us reckoned that she was probably nearer 35.) Dissatisfied with Maggie's solitary prowess at the helm, Andy partnered her with Tom Ferrie, thus allowing the show to be given its originally planned title.

Tom – up until now star of the Queen Margaret Students' Union where he'd been king of the turntables for many years – had initially joined to host two of the 8 till 10 evening shows. But his personality and talent made him a natural for daytime, and as I write some 36 years later, he is still to be heard every day on Clyde 2.

The latter part of the afternoon was, frankly, a bit odd. At four, bearded journalist Colin MacDonald hosted a 15-minute compilation of comedy records with the stunningly unoriginal title of

Moody publicity shot of Richard Park. Note the cigarette. Smoking was cool in those days.

Three rookie DJs ... Tony Currie, Maggie Cockburn and Dave Marshall.

Tom Ferrie.

Colin MacDonald at the mixing console in
Studio B.

'Cuddly' Kenny Page.

'Have a Laugh'. It had the air of something included in the
franchise application to impress the IBA that we weren't just going
to play non-stop pop records. Colin skilfully hacked these
programmes together from old comedy records (some very old) and
he wandered into the studio from time to time clutching reels of
tape for transmission.

He was followed at 4.15 by small, wiry Kenny Page with another
IBA 'Brownie points' show – 'Ken's Korner.' With a title
reminiscent of an all-night corner shop, it was actually a 15-minute
childrens' programme. Kenny was a risk-taker who lived constantly
on the edge, and although only 19 had the air of one set to go
places. Some days he played records – four to be exact – and some
days he offered excited youngsters their chance to be
a 'DJ for the day'. They got to play two records –
and Kenny chose the other two!

Then it was my turn: 'Homeward Bound' with
the teatime show until 6.30. I reckon I was given the
slot on the strength of my 'proper' demo tape for a
teatime show. Dave Marshall's was for a Breakfast
Show. Now why hadn't I thought of doing that?

I never wanted anything other than to be on
radio or TV. I had decided that when I was four.
By the age of 11, I had built a working radio studio
in my attic and school friends would pop in to
wind up the clockwork gramophones and play
records. My family were the obligatory listeners.

Chums from those days included Dave Marshall, John
MacCalman and Kenny Page as well as Steve Wright, who was yet
to start on the road to super-stardom and at this point held down
a job as a humble clerk with the BBC gramophone library in
London.

By the age of 18 I ran an almost full-time radio station – Radio
Six, so-called after the number of my house on the street – heard by
the residents of an old people's home, wired in next door. Prior to
joining Clyde, I had been given the chance to host a monthly heavy
Euro-rock show for radio station KPFK in Los Angeles, then, as
now, the most powerful FM station on the west coast of the USA.
The show was taped in my mate's bedroom and sent to L.A. where
I was later informed it was so popular they played it every week
until a new one arrived! Visiting KPFK many years later, I was
flattered to discover they still had all my tapes carefully preserved
on their shelves!

Knowing the basics of radio technology meant I was also offered a role in Radio Clyde's engineering department. So after an eight-hour shift as a presenter, I would then take on an eight-hour technical shift, operating the studio control desk for the likes of Frank Skerret, Glen Michael, Don Cumming, Jim MacLeod, Arthur Montford, not to mention the bold AP himself.

Every evening, I was followed on the air by Alex Dickson's grand half-hour 'News Special.' Its main objective seemed to involve as many voices in the studio at the same time as was humanly possible. Alex believed that the best way to prove to the world that we were better than the BBC was to provide convincing proof that we employed more people!

Whilst obviously not the case, Alex somehow created a willing suspension of disbelief in listeners' minds sufficient for the illusion to take root.

The music studio – constructed to house

News and Current Affairs supremo, Alex Dickson.

a small band, a pop group or a handful of actors – would be filled to overflowing with not only every available journalist, but also secretaries, sales folk and even Ruby the switchboard queen. Rosie McNeill, the cleaner, was known to wander in to empty the studio bin while the show was on the air. Nobody seemed to mind.

The microphone table in the studio was small, so those not immediately due to give their live report stood in ranks at the back, making it look for all the world like a dole queue. The other departments viewed this nightly performance with much amusement, but Dickson was deadly earnest.

When Alex was otherwise engaged – as a reservist he often 'buggered off' to play war games – his deputy, Tom Steele, produced 'News Special'. Tom had his own set of idiosyncrasies. He had the disarming habit of battering his head against walls, windows, doors or filing cabinets whenever anything went wrong. 'You're ruining my show!!!' he would intone whilst attempting to pulp his brains against the studio door. How they still continued to function we were never sure.

On Tuesdays and Thursdays I was relieved half-an-hour earlier when veteran broadcaster and journalist Cliff Hanley hosted a half-hour phone-in from six o'clock. 'Heckle Hanley' was live and totally dangerous. Phone-ins were in their infancy in 1974 with Clyde being one of the pioneers of this now ubiquitous genre. The Independent Broadcasting Authority had insisted that we must use a seven-second delay so that we could 'dump' abusive callers before they ever hit the airwaves.

Heath Robinson would have been proud of the mechanism to create this delay. One of our tape recorders was fitted with an enormous deck and a baffling number of wheels and pulleys. The tape would be threaded around all of these in such a way that it took seven seconds to pass from the record to the playback head – thereby creating a suitable delay. The whole thing was bizarre and unworkable and nobody ever bothered to use it. (Some years later I discovered that BBC Radio Manchester had used a large plant pot and a pencil to achieve the same effect. Think about it.)

Thus Cliff's callers heckled live. Unexpurgated. One youth rang from Dumbarton. Cliff's producer, Karin Spalter (an uber-elegant lady who seemed to produce just about everything that came out of the news department) put the caller through to Mr Hanley.

'My next caller is in Dumbarton. By the sea. Ach, I can almost smell the salt water from here. You're through to Heckle Hanley. What would you like to discuss this evening?'

'Fuck off, Hanley!'

'An erudite if pointless comment. Thank you for paying for the call. Who's next?'

Nothing ever fazed Cliff. The show carried on regardless. Nobody said a word afterwards.

Evenings were a heady mixture of speech and music in the good old BBC Light Programme tradition. As the station grew, more speech programmes appeared in the early evening and I often found myself panel-operating (and frequently producing by default) Malcolm Mackenzie's education programme 'Notice Board', Sheila Duffy's consumer show and the political programme 'Clyde Comment' presented at first by Tom Steele, then George Reid, then Donald Dewar.

Lanky Donald, whose knowledge of all things impressed me greatly, and who was enormous fun to work with, would – like the others – communicate with me using crude sign language. As we both sat in the same studio with no soundproof separation (unlike the BBC) instructions to each other had perforce to be silent. A rather rude gesture with the left hand placed in the joint of the right while folding the right arm was used to indicate the imminence of a commercial break, and the future First Minister's political guests were often startled when he made such gestures while they were in the middle of a political rant; more so when he would leer at me with a threatening cut-throat gesture – in reality simply indicating his desire to ditch a particular telephone caller.

Later evenings also included some specialist music – 'Folk and Suchlike' with woolly-hatted expert Drew Moyes, and 'Country Sounds' with the knowledgeable Bill Black whose subsequent career as a country DJ has been enormously successful. Onetime *Melody Maker* guitarist of the year, Ken Sykora was already a household name as presenter of 'Roundabout' on the old BBC Light Programme. He popped up to host 'The Big Bands' and a late-night show 'Ken's College of Useless Knowledge'. Scots songwriter Bill Martin ('Puppet on a String') taped a weekly chat show somewhere in London and put it in the mail. We never saw him.

Tom Steele out and about with the radio car.

Former STV continuity scriptwriter John G Temple produced a weekly documentary series tracing the history of Glasgow. 'The Dear Green Place' was the station's only serious attempt at an entertainment feature programme and it was fronted by actor Jimmy Copeland. Some years later, John Temple was to become a respected television figure as producer of 'Coronation Street'.

The rest of the evening was filled with pop, hosted by Tiger Tim on Tuesdays and Thursdays; Brian Ford (real name Brian Ferguson, a stalwart of Edinburgh's hospital radio service and another engineer-cum-presenter) on Mondays and Wednesdays, and 'Cuddly' Kenny Page carving a niche with his new releases show 'Clyde Climbers' on Friday evenings.

At first, these shows continued until 10.30pm, then Dickson decided that a late-evening version of 'News Special' was called for to compete with ITN's 'News at Ten' on the box. The troops were again amassed for an all-night brainstorming session involving Dickson, Steele, me and a box of cakes. We came up – in true newspaper style – with the title 'Late Extra', and I picked title music that sounded remarkably like the theme for 'News at Ten', probably because both pieces were composed by my much admired friend Johnny Pearson. The idea was to replicate the all-singing, all-

Arthur Montford, whose loud sports jackets were replaced for radio with smart sweaters.

dancing teatime magazine, but inevitably by 10pm there were but few folk left in the building (except for Rosie the cleaner of course) so it quickly became just an extended bulletin.

Part of Radio Clyde's early success could doubtless have been attributed to a government-imposed television curfew at 10.30pm. Owing to serious fuel shortages at the end of 1973, some bright spark in the appropriate ministry came up with the notion that by closing all television down at that time, the nation would be forced into going to bed early therefore using less energy.

Whether this ever had the slightest effect on the fuel resources or not I have no idea (although I suspect the birth rate might have gone up a bit) but it did unexpectedly deliver a huge audience to Radio Clyde at a stroke. With no telly at night, and commercial time at only £1.50 for a 15-second spot, the public and advertisers alike turned to the new radio in droves, to be entertained by Iain Anderson, Don Cumming, Frank Skerret, Glen Michael and their individual blends of easy listening music. On Fridays Steve Jones hosted his rock show – of which more later. Many listeners stayed with us after midnight for the late-night shows that continued until 2am.

The weekend mixture was varied to include sport, album charts, the Radio Clyde 'Top Thirty', and in addition to an assortment of repeats of the specialist music shows there was classical music, arts and a Sunday lunchtime request show clearly modelled on the BBC's hugely popular 'Two-Way Family Favourites'. Our version, Radio Clyde 'Worldwide' neatly started half-an-hour before the BBC's, while Radio 2 broadcast a church service!

Glen Michael was the first presenter of the show, but by the summer I took over from him to handle the 200 letters and cards it brought in every week. I am sure that then the BBC employed teams of secretaries and production assistants to cope with this kind of load (although it's a lot leaner an organisation nowadays), but at 261 there was just me and Annie Wood. Since I was also presenting and producing the classical music hour later on

The production team at work in the canteen - John Temple, Eva Flannery, Norman Ross and Annie Wood. The inset is John MacCalman.

Sunday evenings, and Annie had all the other shows to worry about, it was something of a minor miracle that 'Worldwide' got put together at all!

It might have seemed curious for a 'pop' DJ like me to also be presenting the classical programme, and indeed Andy Park was sometimes concerned that my credibility with the audience might be somewhat stretched, especially on those occasions when I additionally stood in for Kenny Page on 'Clyde Climbers'. But the truth is that I have a passion for all kinds of music. I'm as comfortable with Elgar as I am with the Eagles, and I especially enjoyed the weekly hour of classics. Before Clyde launched, Andy had put me in charge of researching the classical programmes and I'd set up some of the presenters – like Iain Turpie – for the first weeks of the programme's life. But Jimmy Gordon was – as always – keen to make the station as accessible to the ordinary listener as possible, so my approach to classics was that although I was no expert, I could perhaps come up with a way of presenting some of the finest music ever composed that was less patronising and stuffy than that of the BBC's Third Programme.

The author pictured in Studio A.

Strangely, for a radio anorak like me, I'd hardly ever tuned in to the aforementioned service, so I came fresh to the 'Popular Classics' with no preconceptions of how to 'do' that kind of show. With the programme scheduled for 6pm on Mondays, immediately after 'Homeward Bound', listeners were led naturally into it and the programme proved to be exceedingly popular. I suspect that it – and its brethren on commercial radio stations elsewhere – created the model for Classic FM in the future.

So although it came as a surprise to many that when I finally left 261 for television I retained my weekly classical hour for a further six years, it was – to me at least – quite logical. And very enjoyable. The afternoon I spent each week researching and choosing the music and writing the scripts was probably the best relaxation I ever got!

The overall pattern of Clyde's programmes seemed to appeal greatly to the punters and from the word go, the station's success was assured. Some of Andy Park's programme ideas were pure dead brilliant. Resurrecting 'McLaughlin's Ceilidh' was surely one of the

The Laird o' Coocaddens himself –
Jack McLaughlin.

best. Jack McLaughlin was already a legend. A former school teacher turned pirate DJ, he made his name on board Radio Scotland as an extrovert entertainer. Tommy Shields had instructed Jack to present the station's nightly programme of Scottish country dance music, to Jack's great horror! Our Jack fancied himself more as more of a mid-Atlantic pop host (the self-styled 'Yak MacFisheries – your lovable ludicrous one') and reckoned there was no way he'd spend the rest of his days playing tartan kitsch. So on his first night he sent the whole thing up.

'Greetings hoochter-teuchter friends in buts 'n' bens, single ends. Shoogle yer sugarally water, lift up yer kilts, and swing to the best in music from north of the haggis line!'

To an audience hitherto accustomed to the measured and deferential tones of the BBC's announcers this was nothing short of anarchy on the air. And they loved it. Tommy Shields did not, however, and instructed that McLaughlin should never present the show again.

Jack's little plan worked – until the mailbags came in with a deluge of enthusiastic letters demanding his immediate reinstatement on the show.

'McLaughlin's Ceilidh' thus became one of the most original and successful shows on any of Britain's pirate stations. When Radio Scotland was forced off the air by government legislation, Jack went on to become a television personality with Aberdeen station Grampian TV. He had also worked with Andy Park on a BBC radio series, and Andy grasped the opportunity to lay hands on a proven success even before Clyde was on the air.

'McLaughlin's Ceilidh' was at first placed on a Sunday night at 10pm, but before long it gravitated to its natural home at teatime on Saturday and was extended to Edinburgh's Radio Forth as well. Indeed so popular was it that STV then picked up the idea and gave Jack his own hour-long telly show, 'Thingummyjig', leading to stage versions touring the country into the bargain. In short, Jack spent the rest of his broadcasting life playing tartan kitsch. No wonder he retired from the media at the age of 40!

Kenneth McKellar had been an icon of my childhood. My father had never shared my passion for buying records, and probably only ever went into a record shop a dozen times in his life. Three of those were to buy Kenneth's records. The tiny handful of EPs that I would pour over as a little boy depicted the dapper Mr McKellar in full highland evening dress.

I had already made up my mind that the first record I would

play when the station opened simply had to be Ken's recording of 'Song of the Clyde', and that was even before I'd discovered that he was a shareholder. It was a real thrill to be able to record an interview with him a few days before opening night, but a much bigger thrill was still to come.

Scotland's best known tenor had many hidden attributes. For one, he was a motorbike fanatic, donning leathers to zoom about the countryside. Rather different from his douce image on my EP sleeve! But even more remarkable was that he wrote comedy scripts under a pseudonym. Not just any old comedy scripts – he contributed sketches to 'Monty Python's Flying Circus' for goodness sake!

Andy Park knew all this and reckoned it was time the punters saw the other side of Kenneth, so he was given an hour-long Friday night comedy show. Scriptwriter David McKellar (no relation) was flown up from London. David wrote for Frankie Howerd, 'The Frost Programme' and 'The Two Ronnies' amongst many others, and was reckoned to be top of the tree. He and Kenneth put the shows together each week. A few days after Clyde opened, Andy came looking for me.

'TC, you're no bad at funny voices and accents. Nip along to Studio B and gie the boys a hand, eh?'

Thus I found myself in the surreal position of being Kenneth McKellar's comedy feed. In most of the shows there were just the two us in the studio, Kenneth being … well, Kenneth, and me being almost everybody else. Andy would come in and add a few voices as well from time to time. The series was a lot of fun – Kenneth turned out to be engaging company and the scripts gave me ample opportunity to show off my range of silly voices, including, may I say, an impersonation of Ugandan despot Idi Amin, of which I was particularly proud.

Alas, the series came to an abrupt end. Whether Andy had only intended it to have a short run, or the ratings were poor, or it was proving too expensive I never learned. My own contribution certainly cost nothing! But I treasure the couple of episodes of the show I still have on tape. And I never saw that EP sleeve in the same light again!

Kenneth McKellar was already a big star in the mid 1950s.

THE ALTOGETHER GUYS

My colleagues on the wireless waves were an entertainingly diverse bunch. And uniquely in radio circles, there was practically none of the rivalry and nastiness that disc jockeys often exhibit towards their fellow record-spinners. Legendary are the tales from 'pirate' radio days of new releases mysteriously vanishing from one DJ's pile to magically reappear in another's; the trick of ending your show with the record the next guy had planned on starting with – petty jealousies and politics abound in most radio stations. But not at Radio Clyde. At least, not in those early days.

Socially, we drank together, ate together, played together and … well, generally got on like a house on fire, often seeking each other's company in the evenings and at weekends. The 261 family.

Some of the 'family' posing in Studio A a few days before Radio Clyde launched (left to right): Colin MacDonald, Dave Marshall, Annie Wood, Tim Stevens and John MacCalman.

Because we had spent some years in each others' company dreaming of the real thing whilst playing at radio stations in my attic, Dave Marshall was my oldest chum. It's a pity that our shifts were really opposites – he had a 4am start in order to be at Anderston Cross with his brain in gear for 6am; whilst I wasn't really needed until late morning or early afternoon.

Chez Marshall of an evening usually involved much yawning on poor Dave's part, and his wife Barbara and I would find ourselves chatting long after Dave had made an exit for bed at 9pm! Barbara was another former hospital radio presenter, having hosted a classical music show on Radio Paisley, and so had a unique under-standing when it came to her husband's career.

Dave's gentle, unpretentious style made him instantly popular, but I don't think he ever expected to be doing the show forever. Twenty-four years later, at a Radio Clyde reunion dinner I asked him if he'd got used to rising early. 'No, I have not', was the reply! Yet he gained for himself the distinction of presenting the same radio programme for longer than anyone else on the planet. 'I must be doing something right … ' was Dave's typically self-effacing reaction.

The 'Jones Boy' – Steve – came to Glasgow after being turned down by London's newly-launched Capital Radio. We were all well aware that he had already made something of a name for himself at BBC Radio 1, and many of us – being by and large beginners at this radio lark – were in considerable awe of the man. But could a big

The first group photograph. Back row (from furthest left): Ken Macleod, Jimmy Copeland, Jim MacLeod, Maggie Cockburn, Steve Jones, Glen Michael, Richard Park, Jim Waugh, Tony Currie, Frank Skerret, Peter Day, Don Cumming, Brian Ford, Jack Mcaughlin, Colin MacDonald, Iain Anderson and Drew Moyes. Front row: Andy Park, Tim Stevens, Tom Ferrie, Kenny Page, Bill Black and Dave Marshall.

Partying together - Dave Marshall and his wife Barbara, Steve Jones and his wife Lolita. Tom Ferrie appears to have mislaid his wife Nanette ...

bloke from Crewe understand the singular culture of Scotland's largest city?

Sure, he could. Within days he behaved as if brought up here and ironically was the first to skilfully blend records by traditional Scottish country dance music and accordion bands with the likes of Abba and the Rolling Stones. He had been bass player with the Lonnie Donegan band some time before, and Glasgow-born Lonnie had undoubtedly ensured that Steve received a full education in the ways of the city when they'd toured Lonnie's home turf. Before long, we were surprised when newspaper and magazine reporters questioned his Anglo-Saxon origins. Our Steve – English? Surely not ...

Laid back and highly sociable, Steve formed an instant rapport with lunchtime man Richard Park, already a familiar voice from his 'pirate' radio days and BBC Radio 1 gigs. Richard was always heavily into sport, and immediately encountered an embarrassing conflict of interest when his very first late-night 'oldies' show clashed with the Sportsman of the Year Dinner at the Albany Hotel.

No way was he going to miss this one, so before 'Doctor Dick's Midnight Surgery' had even got under way, he wheedled me into deputising on the *very first programme*. The show seemed to go quite well, and a few days later I got my very first fan letter. Obviously an exciting moment, and I savoured it for all it was worth. A pink envelope, delicately-scented and addressed in an unmistakably feminine hand. All a quiver, I opened it and willingly drank in its flattery – 'You're so much better than that Richard Park', gushed its author, adding 'why don't they let you do that midnight show permanently?'

Head swollen and ego dangerously over-inflated I rushed as if still in the school playground to show my prized missive to the other jocks who share the cramped office with me. 'So where's your girlfriend from, then?' queried the Jones boy indulgently. I glanced at the postmark. Kirkcaldy, in Fife; many miles to the east and well beyond our transmission area. Steve threw me a puzzled look. 'Richard,' he called, 'what do you make of this?' as he chucked the pink paper at the rightful occupant of the 'Midnight Surgery'.

'The wee so-and-so ... ' muttered Richard indignantly. The letter was from a certain Miss Park. Richard's wee sister. TC had been well and truly stitched up!

Steve and Richard had a fondness for golf, clubbing and drink – not necessarily in that order – and indulged in these pursuits at every opportunity. Steve had a lengthy spell alone before Lolita and the boys relocated, but Richard often found himself placating his long-suffering (then) wife Brenda from time to time when their adventures inevitably got a bit out of hand.

The good Doctor was greatly at home in his lunchtime slot, balancing the latest chart music with regular trips outside the studio to present the show live from shopping centres, football stadia, exhibitions, or indeed anywhere where the 261 Outside Broadcast Unit could venture and attract sufficient of an audience to make their applause audible.

Adopting a racy and often highly suggestive style, his late-night 'surgery' gave him full rein for naughtiness and *double entendre* whilst chatting up those lucky few who actually got through the

Sporting thier best pullovers in Studio A are Dave Marshall, Steve Jones, Tony Currie and Richard Park.

constantly jammed telephone lines to take part in the show.

A very different kettle of fish was our afternoon girl. Margaret Jane Cockburn was a restless soul, with a bohemian lifestyle. Before coming to us, she'd been working as assistant to a Glasgow University professor. She possessed a rich, sexy voice, making her perfect as a radio pin-up. Petite, with the air of an abandoned puppy, she was the darling of the Altogether Guys, bestowing her affections (and more) generously to practically every male in the building on a strictly controlled timeshare basis. Even those jocks with a natural inclination to seek out sleeping partners of their own sex fell under her spell!

On the air, Maggie's style was on reflection rather more laid back and whispering than an afternoon show demanded. Andy Park gave her a Thursday midnight slot which we unkindly (if accurately) dubbed 'The Wanker's Hours'.

One night when, as had become my habit, I was working late in the building, Maggie had failed to appear by midnight. I slipped into the empty chair and fibbed on air that Ms Cockburn was indisposed. Frantic but futile attempts to get Maggie on the phone made me resort to a casual on-air request that she should perhaps ring the station if she's listening. The duty newsman shot into the studio, paranoid that the tabloids might hear this and – rightly – assume that something was amiss at Anderston Cross Centre.

Eventually Maggie did ring, dozily explaining that, having not slept for several nights in a row, she had taken a handful of sleeping pills around teatime and retired to her bedroom for a nap. The pills had worked just a little too well, and she had stirred around half-past one, hazily aware that she ought to have been somewhere else!

Maggie's flailing solo spot in the afternoons mercifully ended when Andy paired her with the dynamic Tom Ferrie. Tom had been a key part of Glasgow's club scene for many years – indeed many erroneously believed that he'd done a spell on pirate station Radio Scotland, such was his professional style. He was a hit in afternoon, and when Maggie was inevitably gently prised away from the programme completely, its title simply altered from 'Two at Two' to 'Tom at Two'. Neat.

In the early months of 261, I was the solo pilot on the 'drivetime' slot. In the rather bizarre half-hour after Maggie and before 'Homeward Bound' took to the air, there were the two short programmes designed to win what we all dubbed 'Brownie points' with the ruling IBA. Colin MacDonald unashamedly borrowed a format created by wartime bandleader Jack Jackson for 'Have a

Laugh', editing together bits of old comedy records that should somehow hang together. But the resultant mash-up of Tony Hancock, Kenneth Horne, Steptoe & Son and The Goons often made little sense at all!

A demanding and very labour-intensive programme like this inevitably faltered after a few months on the air. MacDonald also fronted a two-hour midnight show on Mondays as well as the Sunday breakfast programme and was only too happy to be relieved of the extra burden. Filling the quarter-hour before my airshift was Kenny Page. His show was a sometimes lacklustre attempt by the bosses to 'cater for the kiddies', and apart from the aforementioned minimal number of current pop records and requests for homework-ridden listeners, his 'young DJs' tended to demand a disproportionate amount of time and effort for the couple of minutes' airtime that they provided.

It's true that he had a special affinity for children. Having been brought up with an extended family in an orphanage, Kenny was without doubt the right man for such a job. But like 'Have a Laugh', 'Ken's Korner' was doomed from the start. Kenny was philosophical when his daily slot got the chop, and focussed his main attention on the Friday evening two-hour show 'Clyde Climbers'. He was also given the task of pinch-hitting for absent jocks, (today he'd have been branded 'swing jock') acting as a production assistant, answering calls during phone-ins and generally making himself useful. All this for a princely £1,300 a year!

Alas, the highly-strung Kenny often allowed himself to be seriously wound up by his bosses, and was once found clinging to the window-ledge outside Andy Park's office after attempting to break in to raid Andy's files and find out if he was the lowest-paid jock on the station. (He was). His daredevil shuffle along the narrow ledge that led from his own office was rendered futile when Park decided to visit his own office at just the wrong moment. Mercifully, Andy saw the funny side of the escapade, and Kenny was subjected to nothing worse than a lashing – of the tongue.

Come the first reshuffle, Andy had decided that my choice of music was perhaps a little too eclectic for a late afternoon, a view clearly shared by our listeners. Richard Park was brought in to host the

A Radio Tay publicity shot of Kenny, taken after he left Clyde for the Dundee station.

Kenny Page

Radio TAY

Brian Ford.

4–5.30pm segment, leaving me to my own devices for the post-news part of the programme until 7.30pm. Although my airshift shrank from three hours a day to 1 hour 40 minutes, I was given the consolation prize of the Sunday lunchtime international request show Radio Clyde 'Worldwide'. I rather suspect that it had more than a little to do with the fact that I cost nothing in comparison with the experienced and well-known Glen Michael. Coupled with a weekly classical music programme, and daily technical shifts, this was more than enough to keep me busy round the clock.

Nowadays, most commercial stations rely on the absolute minimum number of on-air presenters. Radio Clyde in 1974 had the opposite philosophy. During the year there were eight regular daytime presenters, and the number of freelancers and production staff covering evenings and weekends ran to a staggering 22! Our share of larger-than-life characters was immense. Leaving the news and current affairs team for the next chapter, evening presenters included pop jocks 'Tiger Tim' Stevens – who rapidly became the station's number one heartthrob – and technician-turned-presenter Brian Ford (changed from his real name Ferguson in order to 'match' some American radio jingles he'd acquired along the way).

Former newspaper columnist Frank Skerret brought his pawky sense of humour with him, as well as a large dose of vanity and a bevvy of middle-aged lady fans, who would dutifully sit admiringly in the studio, quietly cooing as he delivered his carefully-scripted ad-libs to the microphone.

Musically his stint drew from the 'standards' of performers like Frank Sinatra, Nat 'King' Cole, Peggy Lee and suchlike, and aimed to please the much older audience for whom the Top 40 was anathema. A steady and ever-heavier mailbag indicated that within his target audience, he was a sure-fire hit. His passion for Ethna Campbell's cloyingly-sentimental recording of 'The Old Rugged Cross' knew no bounds, and, to judge from the number of times the selfsame Ethna sat silently beside him in the studio, neither did his passion for the lady herself.

Frank's fondness for a select studio audience of lady admirers evidently wasn't shared by his wife, and one evening I answered the ex-directory private line in Studio C to be find a stressed-out Skerret. Apologetically, he confessed that he physically couldn't

Frank Skerret.

leave the house to present his show that evening, as his wife was clinging firmly to the bumper of his car and point-blank refusing to let go of it.

The mental picture of Mrs Skerret grimly hanging on to Frank's bumper kept me going as I mouthed more fabrications about 'indisposed' presenters and resigned myself to another 90 minutes of unpaid overtime. At least I didn't have to play Ethna Campbell.

Former Scottish Television publicity man turned television director Don Cumming contributed 90 minutes every Tuesday night. Easy-going, freewheelin' Cumming, whose Canadian accent belied the fact that he was Scots-born and educated, entered the studio every Tuesday evening armed with a box of his favourite records and a half-bottle of Scotch. By midnight both were empty.

A year or so after Clyde went on the air, I became Don's next-door neighbour, and I was always grateful that his endearingly happy on-air persona was mirrored in real life. Dear Don never sounded as if he was working when he was on the radio.

Ethna Campbell.

Also from STV came Glen Michael (born Cecil Buckland) whose past life as an actor and comedy stooge left him with an impeccable sense of timing and a brilliant imagination. However, his pivotal role as the sole presenter of every kid's most favourite TV cartoon show, 'The Glen Michael Cavalcade', unfortunately seemed to be matched by a firm, if concealed, dislike of other people's weans. Poor Glen was regularly required to turn up at custard-and-jelly-encrusted parties, and not only smile at the little beggars but blow up balloons for them and generally be nice. He wasn't really comfortable with it, and was always most at home in the secure confines of a studio where his ideas could spring to life.

Often, I would be scheduled to act as Glen's right-hand, operating the equipment while he concentrated on the words. This was one of the best bits of the week. I metamorphosed into his 'feed' (long before it became *de rigueur* for DJs to fill their studios with acolytes), culminating in a magical Christmas night when listeners tuned in to hear the pair of us enjoying the time of our lives as guests at a glamorous and exciting live Christmas party. In reality, we were alone at 10pm on 25 December in a harshly neon-lit studio in Anderston Cross Centre,

The affable Don Cumming.

Jim Waugh.

armed only with a plate of cold chicken legs, a box of Christmas Crackers, a pile of sound-effects records and Glen's infinite imagination. Fortunately, that's all we needed ...

Indeed our working relationship endured after my departure for telly a couple of years later, and Glen would periodically invite me to guest on 'Cavalcade', perhaps the greatest of all privileges in my subsequent television career!

Specialist music demanded specialist presenters – like the delightful Jim Waugh, who presided over 'The World of Jazz' with such wit and aplomb that some years later he became a daily fixture on the west of Scotland airwaves.

Andy Park poached former BBC musician/producer Bob MacDowall from Queen Margaret Drive, and as well as supervising the production of Clyde's wide range of live music sessions (and eventually a series of albums specially produced for sister stations to use), he hosted a Saturday-evening brass band programme under the pseudonym of Bob Mason.

One time intelligence officer, Ken Sykora already had a distinguished broadcasting career with the BBC on the Light Programme, Network Three, Radio 2 and even Radio 1. Born in London, his mother was the stepdaughter of a Swiss-German count who had eloped with a Czech cavalry officer. Ken led his own band in the 1950s, and for five years on the trot was voted Britain's top guitarist by readers of *Melody Maker*. Now semi-retired and running the Colintraive Hotel in Argyllshire, he'd travel to Glasgow once a week to record a couple of shows, including 'The Big Bands'. With a musical knowledge second to none, and a record collection to match, I always felt very privileged to work with such a legend and enjoy his tales of the music business. All the more so when he got into the habit of staying with Karin and me overnight after his midnight show and we could share a nightcap and a blether at three in the morning.

Another former hospital radio colleague (the place was hotching with them), Norman Ross, augmented his income from Caterpillar Tractors with a weekly hospital request show recorded down in the wards. He also invented the irritatingly awful catch-phrase 'Hullo Norman' uttered by some dreadful urchin he had discovered on his travels. For just half-an-hour on the air he became disproportionately famous, with 'Hullo Norman' haunting him for the rest of his life.

Urbane drama lecturer Iain Anderson presided over his ambitiously eclectic 'Anderson Folio' on Monday nights, complete with poetry readings and breathtakingly obscure records. He also hosted the weekly arts magazine 'Interact' which, although a mere half-an-hour to begin with, seemed to take the whole week to record. More of that later.

And as well as tolerating his revived celebration of kitsch tartanalia, Jack McLaughlin also fronted a Sunday morning show in which he interviewed a live studio guest. Since this took to the air immediately before the 'Worldwide' request slot I usually 'drove' the panel for him – purely in the interests of sociability so that he could sit at the 'chat table' (a brown baize-covered hexagonal table, specially designed to be acoustically perfect for a radio studio) and look his guests straight in the eye rather than peer at them awkwardly from behind the 'flight deck'.

Hullo Norman!

Poor Craig Davis held the record for shortest time with the station. Unlike Ben Harris, Craig at least made it to the air with his show at 3.30pm on our first Sunday afternoon. Alas, Andy took exception to his style of delivery and Craig's debut show turned out to be his last. But it made no difference to his following in the city's clubs and his local stardom remained untarnished by his brush with radio.

Jim MacLeod would drop in once a week to tape his 'Nice 'n' Easy Listening Show'. He had a full time job working for Reo Stakis as entertainment manager at Dunblane Hydro and of course fronted his own very successful country dance band whose records sold like hot cakes. Jim could take a while to tape his show as he was prone to errs and umms, but we always edited these out before transmission. Unfortunately, one of the technicians thought it a great wheeze to keep these and string them all together as

Hello, you out there! Iain Anderson.

"The Nice and Easy Listening Show"

Jim MacLeod

Publicity postcard for Nice 'n' Easy Jim MacLeod.

Simon Moore aka Tony Meehan in 242 days.

part of the tape to be played at the station's Christmas party. As soon as he heard this, Andy Park was minded to dispense with Jim's services since he was taking up too much editing time! But fortunately good sense eventually prevailed and Jim stayed where he was.

Ken MacLeod was yet *another* ex-hospital radio colleague. Sales manager of a Glasgow car firm, Ken hosted the Sunday morning show with warmth and humour.

The name 'Simon Moore' disguised the real identity of the evening pop music DJ. His voice would have been familiar to fans of pirate Radio Scotland, for he was really Tony Meehan, ('TM in the AM') but since he was keen to hide his dual role from clients of the successful PR agency he had established since leaving the ship, he picked two of the names associated with 'The Saint' – Simon Templar and Roger Moore. Dear knows why.

From time to time, others would appear briefly on the scene to deputise for holidaying presenters, although fiscal prudence demanded that wherever possible one of us simply 'doubled-up' for a week or two.

Steve Jones once had hit singer Ralph McTell as his deputy; managing director Jimmy Gordon himself filled Frank Skerret's empty chair and when Maggie Cockburn was away, her half of the 'Two at Two' show was taken by Vivien Small, a vivacious young lady not long out of drama school. She subsequently married chief engineer John Lumsden, and came back some years later, as Viv Lumsden, presenting the AA traffic reports during Dave Marshall's 'Breakfast Show' before moving on to become one of the nation's best known television personalities.

Generally speaking, the inhabitants of the news and current affairs department were heavily discouraged from thinking of themselves as DJs. As Head of News, Alex Dickson inclined to the belief that DJs were as plentiful as cherry blossom, and the journalists were encouraged to consider us lesser mortals whose sole purpose was to 'fill time between the news bulletins'.

One reporter, however, displayed worrying signs of talent. Former *Scottish Daily Express* snapper George Montgomery had taken to ringing up Tiger Tim whilst on the air, and putting his talent for impressions of movie stars to unexpected use. Tiger often found himself at the receiving end of phone calls from George Raft, or Humphrey Bogart during his pop show.

We persuaded Andy Park that during Colin MacDonald's four-week summer vacation, the Sunday breakfast show should be handed over to Monty. George was suitably excited about the prospect of being allowed two hours consecutive airtime rather than two minutes, and made grand plans for his four programmes. I even have the mildly embarrassing recollection of singing a little jingle for a trailer to promote his summer spectacular.

On the morning of the first, I was rudely awakened from slumber by the urgent ringing of my bedside telephone at the unearthly hour of a quarter to seven. 'Tony, it's George' intoned a clearly frantic voice, 'the technical operator hasn't turned up for work – neither has the duty newsreader. I'm all alone and I haven't a clue how to put the station on the air. Help!!!'

One amazingly swift taxi ride later, and I was in Studio A putting Clyde on the air and extending as calming an influence as possible on poor Monty who had visions of his career as a record spinner evaporate before his eyes. While the discs played, I'd rush into the newsroom and do my best to cobble together an 8am bulletin. Confused listeners tuned in that morning to hear newsreader George Montgomery presenting the show and DJ Tony Currie reading the news!

As it turns out, the errant technician and newsreader having been to the same party the night before, had woken up simultaneously on the floor of their host's flat nursing hangovers and guilt in equal measure. A week's suspension was their punishment.

Viv Lumsden at the microphone.

George Montgomery working in one of the 'news booths' where journalists edited and recorded their stories.

5 THE NEWSROOM STORIES

The newsroom was right next door to the entertainment department, but it could have been in another galaxy, considering the limited level of official communication between the two departments. This stemmed from Alex Dickson's singular view of the world. An able and distinguished newspaperman, Dickson had come to broadcasting via Scottish Television, where he'd been a regular fixture on channel ten screens for some years as presenter of the evening news magazine 'Scotland Now', predecessor to 'Scotland Today'. Dickson – as Head of News and Current Affairs – was engaged in a permanent state of civil war not only with the entertainment, sales and engineering departments, but also with his own employees. He didn't suffer fools gladly. And in his eyes, it seemed, we were all fools.

His management style relied extensively on the art of the pithy insult. And Alex was especially skilled in this art. Extraordinary memos, sometimes stretching to six or seven pages, flowed effortlessly and eloquently from his battered typewriter. His female

The original news team pictured a few days before Radio Clyde's opening. Left to right: Charles Fitzgerald, Valerie Petit, Richard Roy, Christine Brisbane, Craig Samet, a news secretary who didn't stay long and whose name I never knew, Paul Murricane, George Mackintosh, Bob King, George Montgomery, Tom Steele. Seated in the centre is Sheila Duffy with Alex Dickson to the right.

employees were reduced to tears on a regular basis. He played on the mens' insecurities and since most were on contract, the permanent threat of non-renewal was his nuclear weapon. His armadillo-like hide repelled any protests.

He and Andy Park could never have been described as soul mates, Park regularly reminding him that the airtime for which he was responsible represented but a tiny percentage of the whole. Dickson would counter with abusive and often demeaning remarks about the music presenters, insisting that trained chimpanzees could do their jobs and that journalism was the reason why the good folk of the west tuned in to 261. This was strange as he often appeared to have an even lower opinion of his own people than of Andy's!

In fact, he had picked a fascinating cast of characters. His right-hand woman Sheila Duffy had previously worked with him at STV, latterly presenting the afternoon news programme 'Scotland Early' and was with him from the start. Duffs was always a dependable journalist, with an experienced voice, and a keenly developed estimation of her own worth. She was not a lady to trifle with. As well as reading the main bulletins, she also presented a number of programmes and features in her fuzzily-defined role as 'Women's Editor'.

Although, along with Joan McIntosh she co-hosted the advice

'Consumer Concern' takes to the road for a live OB from the Modern Homes Exhibition in the Kelvin Hall. I don't know the identity of the lady sitting with her back to the camera, but the other backs are (L to R) Muriel Clark, Joan McIntosh and Sheila Duffy, sitting under a large photograph of Tom Ferrie. As usual, John MacCalman is running the desk. The wee curly haired bloke in the foreground is me!

Joan McIntosh.

programme 'Consumer Concern' (later retitled 'Citizens' Advice' for no obvious reason), she became best known to listeners for her daily recipe spot during the Steve Jones Show, bantering with the Jones boy and offering a myriad of mouth-watering goodies.

In fact, she rarely set foot in Studio A, instead taping a whole batch of recipe spots, banter and all, in one afternoon, sometimes doing little to conceal from the technical operator her ill humour at having to undertake such a menial task.

Fiona Ross came with interesting credentials. The daughter of Willie Ross, former Labour Secretary of State for Scotland, she had been a drama teacher and an air hostess prior to joining the 261 team. With finely-tuned political antennae, and a healthy cynicism about everything and everybody, she became known as 'Mrs Mince' due to her habit of describing statements with which she disagreed as 'a load of mince'.

Prominent – for all the wrong reasons – amongst the reporters was Irishman Charles Fitzgerald, known to all as 'Fitz'. Although supposed to be a general reporter, he anointed himself 'Opera and Racing Correspondent', and often the host of the evening pop show would be perplexed to find Fitz in the studio demanding that Led Zeppelin's latest disc be faded down immediately in order that he might read his self-penned review of that evening's performance by Scottish Opera! He also possessed a most unsavoury dog which went by the wholly inappropriate monicker of 'Duchess'.

Duchess would be placed on the chat table whilst her master intoned his words of great import to the nation. For reasons best known to Alex and Andy, Fitz acquired an entire half hour to himself on Saturday afternoons for a programme he dubbed 'The Punter's Choice'. This oddity, although notionally dedicated to the science of the racecourse, often deviated into record reviews, or Fitz offering his own slant on that day's news, assisted as always by the malodorous Duchess.

One spring day, Fitz found himself scheduled to cover the launch of a new ship from one of the Clydebank yards. This was singularly inconvenient, since he had persuaded some hapless PR hack at British Rail into giving him a free rail pass to travel around the North of Scotland for the long weekend. Alas, the launch was scheduled for Friday lunchtime. His free passes were dated and thus worthless unless used on the specific Friday. The ship would be

Fiona Ross with the 261 Radio Car.

launched come what may, so our man had no alternative but to provide a suitably impressive commentary. Such a dilemma might go unresolved by a lesser mortal, but not so Charles Fitzgerald.

On the morning of the day before the launch he collected one of the two radio cars, vehicles equipped with a small on-board radio studio and a giant mast and radio transmitter, allowing live interviews and reports to be fed into the programmes from virtually anywhere in the 261 transmission area. At lunchtime, he duly provided a colourful live commentary of the launch during the main 1pm news bulletin. Then he returned the car to its garage and beat a hasty retreat to the safety of his flat. To pack?

Later that evening, Alex was enjoying a nippy sweetie in his regular – the BBC Staff Club, naturally – when his opposite number at BBC Radio Scotland wandered in with an air of resentment. 'How did you buggers know that bloody boat was launched a day early?' he demanded.

'Sorry?'

'You must have been really on the ball to get your man out there so fast. We still haven't been told that the launch was brought forward.'

'Er, yes … '

Immediate enquiries revealed the boat to be still cosily berthed in Clydebank. In a display of breathtaking chutzpah, Fitz had simply driven the radio car to the nearest hilltop, set up the mast and delivered an impressive commentary entirely from his own imagination. He was fired.

Alex Dickson takes up the story …

'The following Sunday morning, Fitz arrived at the office in his Sandeman hat and cape-overcoat (à la Orson Welles), asked me if I was serious, then drew off one of his gloves, finger by finger, and whacked me across the face with it, demanding satisfaction.

'I used up my store of four letter words and he was bundled off the station. Several hours later, mid-afternoon, when I went to the car park, he leapt out of the gloom and jumped on me. For several minutes two grown men rolled around in the dust. Inconclusively, and no blood, but it got it out of his system.'

After the main news programme – 'News Special' – at half past five, most of the news team would head for the conviviality of the Cabin Bar, leaving just a couple of their colleagues behind to look after the rest of the evening's summaries. On one such occasion, Fitz (reinstated, of course) was on late duty, his main task being to compile a ten-minute news bulletin to be broadcast at 10pm. 'Late

Charles Fitzgerald.

Special' generally included a wide variety of spoken news reports, pre-recorded on tape and subsequently transferred onto cartridges, allowing the technical operator to shove them into the machine and play them instantly without any prior need to find the right spot on a reel of tape. The duty newsman was expected to select these reports, transfer them to 'carts' in a little booth adjacent to the newsroom, and carefully label each tape. Unfortunately, Fitz was in the throes of organising his marriage.

At this point he was unsure whether he wanted to be hitched in Glasgow Cathedral, Studio B, or a ship at sea. Consequently, all evening he was permanently on the phone to a bizarre assortment of officials, wheedling for special permission to do ... well, almost anything that common punters wouldn't be allowed to.

Come five minutes to ten and Fitz had paid no heed whatsoever to the impending bulletin. The clock on the wall eventually wormed its way into his consciousness, and he suddenly grabbed half-a-dozen blank 'carts' from the box, sticking hastily-scribbled labels on them and sprinting through to the news studio, stopping only to hand them to Dave Murricane in the control room, whose job it was to start the tapes on a spoken cue from the newsreader.

The theme music played.

'Good Evening, this is Late Special and I'm Charles Fitzgerald. The Prime Minister made an important speech at the Tory Party Conference in Brighton today. Ed Boyle now reports.'

Silence ...

'I'm sorry. We don't seem to have that story. In Washington, more problems for the US President as IRN's American correspondent now reports.'

Silence ...

'I'm sorry, we can't seem to raise Washington at the moment. We'll move on to some local news. A bad accident closed the A74 earlier today as George Mackintosh now reports.'

Silence ...

And so it painfully continued, with a nonplussed Fitz apologising each time for the lack of a report. At the end of the bulletin he burst into the control room and yelled at Dave, 'You idiot. You've ruined my news bulletin. I shall see to it that you're fired immediately.'

And, gathering up the evidence he swept back into the newsroom.

He was fired. Again. Indeed, the bold Fitz's dismisals roughly coincided with the phases of the moon.

The wedding eventually came along and was attended by all and an excellent evening it was. The Radio Clyde family was generally very forgiving of its own. Even Fitz.

After Fitz had departed Clyde (and Scotland) for good, a wee lady from the florist's in Anderston Cross presented Alex with a bill for the buttonhole flowers Fitz always wore. She'd been waiting for her money, she said. Fitz had assured her that Clyde was picking up the tab for his flowers and had promised he would do his best to accelerate the station's accounts department. She hadn't wanted to make a fuss and had waited, rather reluctantly. But she'd realised Fitz was no longer at 261 as he hadn't been in for a while and, apologetically, she asked if Radio Clyde would please settle the bill?

It was a not an inconsiderable amount.

Few of Fitz's newsroom colleagues managed to achieve his record for being fired. But to be fair, many tried. One reporter, with a penchant for listening to Hitler's war speeches late at night in one of the editing cubicles, would become intensely irritated with members of the public who foolishly telephoned Radio Clyde after 10pm, since after that time the duty newsman had the additional task of answering the phones. This particular journalist would answer calls with a cheery 'Fuck off and leave me alone' to whomsoever was unlucky enough to have rung Clyde's number. One night, inevitably, it was the managing director. He wasn't fired.

Mike Russell was a stockily built man who had made quite a name for himself as a broadcast journalist. When sober, unquestionably, he was one of the very best of Dickson's men. Unfortunately, he was given to joining his boss for a few wee swallies in the BBC Staff Club of an evening. One such night he made his way unsteadily back to the newsroom around 9.45pm in a disquieting mood, clutching six cans of lager and a bottle of The Famous Grouse.

The 10pm news appeared to be little more than a reshuffling of the stories broadcast at 5.30pm. The midnight news was indeed exactly the same, although his pronunciation was by now becoming slightly eccentric. By this time, it had fallen to me to present the all-night programme running from 2 to 6am (the reason why, you will read later), and it was by and large a most pleasant show to host since practically nobody every strayed near the studio at that time in the morning. Certainly not the Head of Entertainment. And Mike and I had developed a nightly discourse, whereby I would pick up on some item in the 4am bulletin and the two of us would ad lib a discussion on whatever subject I had chosen. It was not our

NOT IN IT FOR THE MONEY

The general view that radio presenters were on big money was of course completely untrue. When I started, my salary was £2,000 a year and like everybody else I was deemed to be self-employed and had a six-month contract for starters. The rates of pay didn't vary much - for presenters the scale went from £4,000 down to £1,300 and only Steve Jones was started on a two-year contract. Newsroom freelances ranged from £3,750 down to £1,400.

Jimmy: 'You're proposing to pay him how much??'

practice to discuss our subject in advance, far let alone rehearse it. Instead it was left to my last-minute discretion. Good seat-of-the-pants broadcasting.

When I went on the air at 2am on this particular morning, Mike's news bulletin was, I fear, largely incomprehensible. It was, therefore, something of a relief when he took his scripts and his large frame lurched back to the safe haven of the newsroom at two minutes past two. Alas, he returned about an hour later, barricaded himself firmly into the news studio and proceeded to relay to my headphones in laborious detail the (largely imagined) great failures of his life. This he did with the aid of the electronic communication system between the studios, thus ensuring that I could neither turn off his ramblings nor hear anything of the programme I was supposed to be presenting at the time.

After 20 minutes or so of this, he mumbled something incoherent and gallumphed back from whence he had come. I rang the security man and asked if, as the only other person in the building at the time, he might perhaps feel inclined to do something about this increasingly serious problem.

'Sorry, son – ah look efter external security – what youse get up tae in here is no ma business.'

Gave me a great big warm glow of comfort, that did.

With much trepidation, I glanced at the clock. Five to four. Mike was due to read the five-minute summary at four. And then our chat. Cripes! At a minute to go, Mike hove into the studio, exhaled a gigantic cloud of alcohol vapour over me and without a word flung his ample frame into the newsreader's chair. What was a poor wee DJ to do? Mike was around 20 stone, drunk as a skunk and evidently dangerous.

I was ten stone, sober and scared.

I took the coward's way out.

I played the news jingle, faded up the big man's microphone and prayed for a miracle.

'Herc'sh the newsh.

'Those baaashtards have shot two of our boys in Norn' Ireland.' (mumble, mumble, bashtards, mumble)

' 'n I don't feel like shaying anyshing elsh ... '

I hurriedly fired the jingle for the end of the news and went into the next record without comment. Mike staggered out of the door still muttering and did not appear again. Half an hour later, the security man rang.

'Ah jist rang tae tell ye yir man's went aff. Sez he's awa' tae fling himsel' intae Hogganfield Loch.' The loch was evidently also beyond the security man's jurisdiction.

We transmitted the 5 and 6am news bulletins direct from LBC in London (as luck would have it, these were read that morning by former STV announcer Douglas Cameron) and once Dave Marshall got himself on the air I rushed through to the newsroom to see what was to be done. The scene was devastating.

Mike had stuffed every one of the newsroom typewriters into metal wastepaper bins; shredded all of the previous day's news scripts; thrown the reels of tape containing news reports from London out of the newsroom window with the yards of recording tape floating in the morning breeze like spring blossoms; ripped all the paper from the teleprinter – in short, he had well and truly trashed the place,

Worse, there was nothing left to squeeze a scrap of news out of for the peaktime 7am bulletin. And anyway there was nobody there to read it.

Well, except for me.

With the help of the unflappable news secretary Rosemary Apartopoulis, who arrived as scheduled shortly afterwards, we extracted whatever we could from the single copy of that morning's *Daily Record*, thoughtfully provided by Rosie, which now constituted Radio Clyde's entire news resources.

Shortly before seven, I worked out how to reload paper in the teleprinter just in time to get a printout of the very last story in the London station's bulletin. It was crap. It was irrelevant. But it was a story, and it was in my hands!

Oddly enough not one single soul subsequently rang to question why a) the lead story dealt inexplicably with the deaths of two gay French ballet dancers or why b) Tony Currie had suddenly become a newsreader.

Mike, meantime, had wandered around for a bit and then – presumably forgetting his suicidal resolve – gone home to bed. He was not fired. Merely suspended for a week. Nobody mentioned the incident to him again, and we resumed our cosy chats after the 4am news as if nothing had ever happened. The newsroom waste bins were, however, never the same again.

Shortly after this incident, I was summoned to the front door early one morning. The security man was perplexed. Two of the boys in blue were at the door with a warrant. And internal security (as we all know) wisnae his problem. Unfortunately, as duty technician, it turned out to be mine. I put on my best sunny smile and ushered in the two detectives.

'And what can we do for you, guys? Record requests, tickets for the Policemen's Ball or ... ?'

'We're from the drugs squad. We've a warrant for the arrest of one of your reporters. Name of David Jarvis.'

David – who was at this time moonlighting as a reporter for one of the best-known Sunday tabloids and was evidently up to his neck in some drugs story – was inconveniently about to read the 8am bulletin. Mindful of previous incidents, I insisted that he was not to be arrested until after he had delivered the eight o'clock to the nation.

Thus two burly policemen were made to sit impatiently outside the studio while I nervously operated the panel for poor David, as he innocently read the news, blithely unaware of what was to come. As the news ended I leant over and addressed him on the intercom. 'David – there are two guys here to see you.' He was handcuffed and marched off. I managed to get a substitute in time for the 8.30 headlines. Whatever David had become involved in, he must have been in it well over his head. He escaped serious incarceration (and wasn't fired) but a few months later was found dead, mysteriously drowned on the first day of his honeymoon.

After a while, it was decided that 'News Special' should be produced in Studio A, rather than the music studio. This was very much a less than perfect arrangement, since it required me to start my closing theme tune, leap out of the chair and allow a technical operator in to line up sometimes as many as 15 pre-recorded news reports, whilst simultaneously setting up the microphones at the chat table for up to six reporters. A recipe for disaster. So naturally one happened.

Craig Samet could sometimes be less than on the ball when it came to knowing which planet he was currently visiting. One evening as the guy in charge of presenting (and, by default, producing) 'News Special' he turned up in Studio A together with technical operator Dave Murricane and a handful of journalists a few minutes before the end of 'Homeward Bound'. My theme tune finished and I punched the button to start the news jingle.

At this precise moment Dave noticed the total absence of any paper. 'Craig – where's the script?'

'Oh, Jeez, I left it in the newsroom. I'll nip through and get it ...'

Craig ambled off, oblivious to the fact that in some 20 seconds' time the news jingle would come to an end and he ought to be reading the first page of the missing script.

Dave threw me a panic-stricken expression. The jingle ended and still no sign of Samet. Dave glanced through the glass to the news studio, where Bob King was ready to read the headlines. He faded up Bob's microphone and cued him to read the news.

I was standing behind Dave, alongside another of the technical operators, Louise Tate, who was patiently waiting to accompany me to the Cabin Bar. By now, Dave was really wound-up by Craig's unprofessional behaviour. As he reappeared through the studio door – a mere 20 seconds too late – Dave, in exasperation and uncharacteristically uttered a stream of unbroadcastable expletives.

It was at this moment that we all became horribly aware that Dave had not actually faded up the newsroom microphone. Instead, he had faded up the one right in front of himself. The one he was shouting into. As shocked realisation of what had happened dawned on us, Louise was the first to react. She grabbed the first jingle to hand and thrusts it into the cartridge player.

'*Have a good morn …* '

That was as far as our jingle singers got.

Louise's choice of the 'Have a good morning' jingle was less than appropriate as it was now nearly six o'clock in the evening. I stopped the tape and removed it from the player, thus neatly compounding the felony and creating more nasty dead air. Ashen-faced, Dave cued Craig who, blissfully unaware of the chaos for which he had been responsible, cheerfully began the programme as if nothing at all remiss had happened and we waited for the switch-board to light up with offended listeners.

Nobody phoned.

We awaited the inevitable round of sackings. Apparently none of the senior management had been listening.

For safety's sake, I quietly let myself into the engineering room, and found to my relief that the incident had been recorded at the very end of a reel of log tape. (It was a legal requirement that the entire output had to be recorded in case the IBA or anybody else needed to check what had been said.) I neatly snipped off six feet of recording tape, and deposited it in the nearest bin.

Honest, Jimmy, the incident never happened …

Weekend bulletins were generally read by the golden-voiced Alastair Dunnett,[2] a veteran newspaperman who had taken the

---

2 Not to be confused with Alastair Dunnett, editor of the *Daily Record* and then *The Scotsman.*

Alastair Dunnett.

decision to end his days in the comfortable billet of editor of *The Campbeltown Courier*. Jimmy Gordon persuaded him not to let his very considerable talents as a broadcaster go totally to waste, so he endured the dreary bus journey from Campbeltown every Friday evening, and then read all of the weekend bulletins, generally returning to a camp bed in the studio after evenings in the Cabin Bar with his colleagues. He had the unnerving habit of reading the Saturday morning bulletins through a hammer-like hangover, clad only in his long Johns!

Early one Saturday, he developed a nosebleed so severe that all the pages of his bulletin became saturated with blood and Steve Krasnow, the engineer on duty, had to fade out Alastair's microphone just seconds before he passed out completely. Alastair was the first of the 261 family to pass away. No doubt his passion for a dram or two helped him on his way, but – when sober – he was one of the most endearing and talented characters in the newsroom and his loss was strongly felt by everyone in the station.

Today it would be unthinkable for a Glasgow radio station not to have a vibrant and thriving sports department, but when Clyde started sport was simply tacked on to the news department. Jim Dolan was our 'official' sports correspondent but the Saturday sports programme soon developed its own network of stringers who could ring in with football match reports. In the studio this was anchored by Richard Park and Bob Crampsey, already a very familiar face from STV's 'Scotsport'. Bob was also a headmaster and former 'Brain of Britain' from the BBC radio series 'What Do You Know?' His knowledge of football (and indeed almost every other subject under the sun) was astounding and he and Richard made a great team on the air. He was also one of the nicest people in the station and an absolute joy to work with.

Bob and Richard fronted the very professional football results and reports part of the Saturday sports programme, but the first couple of hours were something of a mishmash, billed as 'Sportsbag' but known internally as 'Saturday Scrapheap'. Covering sports was expensive, both in human terms, and because of the need to pay rights to sporting organisations for the privilege of live commentaries.

The familiar face of Bob Crampsey as viewers knew him on 'Scotsport'.

The programme was produced by Karin Spalter, who had

joined the station with presenting and production experience at Border TV and STV, especially in news and feature programmes. She produced a range of current affairs programmes, including her own chat show and the Saturday afternoon sports programme. Indeed, she had a responsibility for at least one feature programme every single day of the week. She, together with presenter Paul Murricane and reporter Brian Henson, invented all sorts of – er – 'sports' … like pie-eating contests … or racing home-made dinghies in the Clyde and Forth Canal using Radio Clyde T-shirts as sails.

Or the infamous Shabby Gardens Contest. The idea was Dickson's – its genesis being a wildlife garden feature in *The Observer* Sunday supplement. Listeners were invited to nominate the shabbiest garden in the Radio Clyde area and we'd judge them and award a prize for the worst. Seemed a light-hearted notion. Karin persuaded me to join her in some of the judging, and it quickly became apparent that the contest wasn't going to work. Neighbours with a grudge would send nominations in the hope of settling scores; and one of those nominated was obviously neglected as a result of infirmity or disability on the part of the unfortunate garden owner.

In the end the contest quietly vanished without trace. A pity, since a trophy had already been purchased and engraved. I suspect it's still hiding somewhere in a newsroom cupboard all these years later!

In my role as technician, I was frequently called upon to assist members of the newsroom who ranked among the electronically illiterate. Karin was one of the team who regularly requested my services. It struck me that it would be awfully nice to ask her out, but she clearly didn't see me as her sort at all!

On Christmas Eve 1974, she appeared at my desk with a sob story. Her own conversation programme, 'Social and Personal' was due for transmission that evening, and she had recorded a special edition with well-known actor Iain Cuthbertson. The tape – made on a portable machine – needed quite a few technical adjustments. Since it was a hilarious fantasy concerning the mythical 'Here-we-are Island' that she and Cuthbertson had concocted between them on the spot, it also required bags of musical inserts to make it work.

Would I help? Please? Well, of course!

It took all day and I found myself still editing part one whilst simultaneously presenting that evening's 'Homeward Bound'. And part two was only ready on time by the very skin of its teeth.

Karin Spalter.

Overcome doubtless by relief and seasonal bonhomie, Karin offered to buy me a drink and over our second gin and tonic in the Albany Hotel (upstairs Cocktail Bar, *not* the Cabin) I mentioned casually that the BBC were broadcasting Elton John's live concert that night on TV and in stereo on Radio 1, and that in my flat I had set up all the necessary equipment to enjoy this spectacle to the full. Would she perhaps care to join me? It had an edge of originality over inviting her to see my etchings.

She accepted my invitation.

Six months later ours was the first Radio Clyde wedding. A quiet affair in a tiny church in Old Struan, Perthshire, with news reporter Paul Murricane as my best man, Viv Small as bridesmaid, Paul's twin brother David playing his specially-composed Wedding March on the organ, and Chief Engineer John Lumsden as photographer, bell-ringer and outside broadcast engineer. The guys even brought along the small Outside Broadcast unit to record the event for posterity!

The first Radio Clyde wedding, 3rd June 1975, (left to right): Rev Stewart Borthwick, John Lumsden, Vivien Small, Karin, myself, Paul Murricane, David Murricane.

6 A DAY IN THE LIFE

At this point in the tale, I shall attempt to create the flavour of a typical day at Anderston Cross Centre, although to be frank there was probably no such thing as a 'typical' day!

You may care to picture the layout of the building before I go any further. Radio Clyde occupied the third (top) floor of an office block in Anderston Cross Centre, a dreary new-build complex of shops, offices and tower blocks built on the site of demolished traditional housing on the edge of the City Centre. (It was, in turn, eventually demolished.)

The Radio Clyde offices occupied an L shape, with the entrance doors and reception area at the corner of the L. To the right were the administration offices – starting with MD Jimmy Gordon's office, then Finance Director Norman Quirk; then on the right a large open-plan office that was home to the sales team, and on the left the commercial traffic department (presided over by the gregarious Sheena Russell who had done a similar job for pirate Radio Scotland) with the far end of the corridor occupied by the commercial production studio where the advertisements were made. This was added about 18 months after the station opened, and was the province of Dave Murricane.

Take a left from reception and you were in the production wing. First the all-important canteen, presided over originally by 'Big May', whose culinary ability ran to chips but not a lot else. Then came the offices for production staff. Andy Park and John Lumsden had their offices here; there was a large technical workshop (a permanent Aladin's cave of components, half-built bits of kit and broken tape recorders) and then, at the end of the corridor, the studios (on the left) and the large record library (on the right). There was also a diesel generator to maintain the station's power in the event of a power cut. I don't recall it ever being used.

The studios: Studio A was the main DJ studio with a large table accommodating up to six guests, and a main console for the presenter or technical operator to sit at. This housed a mixing desk,

Studio A. To my right above the turntables are the 'carts' containing station jingles. Behind me are the commercials and in front of me, the desk and paperwork. And an ashtray!

'cart' players, tape recorders, turntables and the main microphone. It was mirrored in the smaller Studio C next door (originally called Master Control) where some of the shows originated, including the 'Through the Night' programme that came along later. For quite some time Studio C had no door, and after I'd joked about this on air repeatedly, one listener sent in a toy plastic doll's house door!

The big music Studio B was at the far end – this had a separate control room and large music recording studio. All the studios had soundproof glass windows so that you could see all the studios from any given one, and adjacent to all three was a News Booth where news bulletins came from.

Friends would often enquire 'if I only turned up for 90 minutes work and then went home'. It wasn't *quite* as simple as that …

At the time of this 'typical' day, I would have been hosting 'Homeward Bound' five evenings a week and providing technical cover for two or three days as well, looking after technical operations for Frank Skerret and the sports programmes on Saturday, and presenting Radio Clyde 'Worldwide' and 'Popular Classics' on a Sunday.

A fairly typical Wednesday would start for me around 10am when I generally breezed into our communal office. The DJs had the assistance of Judith Landless, who not only acted as our PA, but also looked after our incoming (but not outgoing) mail, took telephone messages, organised our diaries and generally acted as mother despite her tender years (she was but a teenager when she started).

After grabbing the first of far too many coffees, I'd check out the morning mail. There would be 50 or so requests for 'Worldwide'. Despite my weekly plea for folk to send their record requests on postcards most ignored the advice and sent letters. Some were indeed lengthy missives, with the actual request buried towards the end of their flowing prose. Annie Wood produced 'Worldwide', but always had a zillion other things to do, so I usually looked after the mailsort myself.

I'd go through all of these with a highlighter pen, marking the

Singer Robin Hall with Karin Spalter in the Control Room of Studio B, working together on their Sony Award-winning documentary, 'The Sing-Song Streets'. More smoking!

bits I planned to read out on the air. From the beginning of the week, I'd have kept a running tally of discs requested. In a two-and-a-half hour show there would be time to play 40 to 50 records, so I had to keep track of the most requested vinyl. A doddle nowadays with a PC to hand, but in the early 70s it was all bits of paper and backs of envelopes. Not even a Post-It note to assist – these were yet to be invented!

After half-an-hour or so sorting out the 'Worldwide' mail, I'd eyeball the rest of the morning's post. Four packets of new singles from different record companies; most of the discs by singers or bands you and I have never heard of. I'd listen to these later. Meanwhile I'd pop my head round the door of the adjoining office to check with Marion (John Lumsden's PA) to see what knob twiddling duties I was booked for.

On Wednesdays I was normally assigned to Studio B (the big music studio) to look after the recording and editing of the weekly arts magazine 'Interact'. Presenter Iain Anderson, obligatory mug of coffee in hand, would be waiting for me, together with some of the team and invariably an ominous-looking pile of tapes of various sizes, plus a few bits of paper. To produce this half-hour speech-based programme demanded a lot of time and concentration. Five of the items might already have been recorded on tape, but four of them could be raw and require editing, both for length (they'd be too long) and for content (some might have mistakes and retakes, some would have sections we had no time to include, some were useless …)

Editing tape is an art form. Today it has been superceded by computer editing which is simple, accurate and very fast. And can be undone. Back in the 70s, it was different. You'd play the tape up to the point where the edit should happen. The tape would be stopped, and by hand you'd 'rock and roll' the tape backwards and forwards over the replay head (emitting the most peculiar noises) until you identified the exact location of the cut. Years of experience gave you the ability to comprehend words and music when played forwards or backwards at speed. The spot was marked on the tape with a soft chinagraph pencil, and then you'd whizz on to the point where you'd want to join the tape. This would involve the same 'rock and roll' process and another chinagraph mark. Then you'd cut the tape, using a special blade and a precision metal groove with an exact angle of 60 degrees allowing every cut to be made at exactly the same angle (otherwise you couldn't join bits of tape together and have them play as if no edit existed). You'd pull away the length of unwanted tape (anything from a couple of inches to several yards) and cut back to the first mark. The unwanted tape went straight into the bin. Then you'd butt the two cuts up against each other in the editing jig, and using a special kind of adhesive tape that didn't ooze adhesive after a while (the way normal adhesive tape does) you joined the two bits of tape together.

Then it would be time to play the edit and see if it worked. Often it didn't and tiny bits of tape would have to be shaved off or grafted back on until the edit sounded perfect. Sometimes a word or just a breath might have to be salvaged from the waste bin. An average edit took two to three minutes to perform. And a half-hour show like this might have 20 to 40 edits in it. Once all the pre-recorded items were edited, they'd be joined together on one spool with bits of coloured leader tape between them to allow the identification of the start of each individual item.

Another coffee and we would be ready to roll. The programme's signature tune was recorded on a 'cart', so that just had to be slotted into the machine, and it would start instantly at the press of a button. Another tape machine (the studio boasted four) had a brand new ten-and-a-half-inch diameter reel of blank tape laced up ready to record the whole programme. These reels were expensive – even in the 70s, blank reels were around £15 apiece.

Off we'd go, with Iain and his colleagues through the glass from me in the studio, reading their contributions, or being interviewed. Now and then Iain would wave his hand to cue one of the pre-recorded items, which I'd play in. While that was playing, the studio microphones were switched off and Iain or one of the team would pop into the control room to give me instructions about what was due to happen next. We rarely worked with a complete detailed script, preferring a more spontaneous approach. (Well, that's what Iain called it …)

Once the whole show was complete, it was often necessary to edit bits of the master recording, taking out fluffs, mistakes, expletives, coughs etc. I also had to accurately time the whole programme, insert a length of yellow spacer tape in the middle where the commercial break would go, (that would be played in live on Sunday, the night of transmission) and put other coloured leaders at the top and tail.

Finally, the paperwork. A sheet for the technical operator on Sunday night, detailing the start and finish of each part and its duration. Then a copyright return, detailing the performers, composers, publishers and record numbers of each piece of music used in the programme. Into the box and another show in the bag.

Time for lunch – into the 261 canteen for something with chips and if there was time, a gossip with some of the others.

After lunch and a quick pint across the road in the Cabin, it would be back to the office to start planning 'Homeward Bound'. At that time we had a completely free choice of which records we played. DJs were chosen partly for their musical knowledge, and were trusted to 'build' and produce their own programmes. So the next stop was always the large record library, presided over by the formidable Miss Fraser. The library held card index lists of everything – 4,000-plus albums and 10,000 or so singles – but I preferred to browse along the shelves when making up a programme. Although I never had a strict format for the programme, I'd usually select tracks in a sequence that would be easy to listen to, so an average programme – would look something like this:

> Theme Tune
> Current chart single – group – upbeat
> Female vocal, album track
> Tonight's weather forecast
> Commercial break
> Male vocal – new release
> AA Traffic report (live from AA headquarters in Erskine)
> Pop instrumental
> Commercial Break
> Golden oldie – group from 1966
> New album track – male vocal
> Chart single – female vocal
> News Bulletin
> Commercial Break

... and so on until the end of the programme. To make all this work I'd need about 35 records, although as the programme progressed I might drop some. The chart singles were all kept in Studio A itself, in a little box at the side of the control desk. I would stagger in to the studio around 4.15 clutching a pile of albums and non-chart singles, together with the weather forecast (which I picked up in the newsroom) and a case containing all of my jingles.

Some of these were my own copies of regular Clyde jingles, but also my own signature tune and some jingles specially recorded for me. In the early days of Clyde, record companies would do

BUYING TIME

Buying advertising time on Radio Clyde wasn't nearly as expensive as some people thought. That was the message that Peter Elliot's sales team took to shops and small businesses across the area every day. A 15-second commercial, broadcast any night after 10pm was a mere £1.60! But that was at the start - as soon as the station proved itself successful, the same spot was then charged at £3.50.

At opening, the most expensive spots were in 'Prime Time' between 6 and 10am on weekdays, 7 and 2pm on Saturdays and 10 and 3pm on Sundays, at a rate of £20 per 30-second commercial. A year later, those times had shifted noticeably - 'Prime' was now 6am - 2pm on weekdays, 7am-2pm Saturdays and 9am-2pm on Sundays, with a 30-second spot increasing to £30, and £40 by July of that year.

By 1977 a national advertiser was being asked for £86 for a 30-second prime spot and a local advertiser £68.50. Overnights were the 'bargain basement' with a 30-second spot going for a mere £1.50 and 15 seconds for a pound. Cheap as a pair of sports socks.

Just how many advertisers ever paid the Rate Card is of course unknown. Deals were always there to be done, but Clyde never made a loss!

PACKAGE PLANS

Subject to availability. Package plans may be booked for a single product or service with spots of the same length.
Spots of longer duration than 30 seconds are pro-rata to the 30 second rate.
Each plan must be completed within seven consecutive days.
Spots will be evenly rotated, vertically within time segments and horizontally across days indicated.

Total Audience

Scheduled Monday to Friday inclusive
20% Prime — 40% 'A' — 40% 'B'

Number of Spots	60 seconds	30 seconds	15 seconds
10	£22.40	£11.20	£8.00
20	£21.60	£10.80	£7.60
30	£20.80	£10.40	£7.20
40 +	£19.20	£9.60	£6.80

Run·of·Schedule

Scheduled Monday to Sunday inclusive.
10% Prime—30% 'A'—40% 'B'—20% Night.

Number of Spots	60 seconds	30 seconds	15 seconds
21 3/day	£16.00	£8.00	£5.60
28 4/day	£15.20	£7.60	£5.30
35 5/day	£14.40	£7.20	£5.10
42 6/day	£13.60	£6.80	£4.80
49+ 7 or more per day	£12.80	£6.40	£4.40

Weekend

Scheduled Saturday 0600 to Sunday 2200
30% Prime—30% 'A'—40% 'B'

Number of Spots	60 seconds	30 seconds	15 seconds
10	£24.00	£12.00	£8.40
20	£22.40	£11.20	£8.00
30	£20.80	£10.40	£7.20

Volume Discount

Volume discount will be allowed on an advertiser's total expenditure, before deduction of agency commission, in a given twelve month period, provided that the period is stated in advance by the advertiser and agreed by Radio Clyde.

Over £5000	2%	£20,000	8%
£10,000	4%	£25,000	10%
£15,000	6%	£30,000	12%
		£40,000	15%

BASIC RATES

All spots will be rotated evenly throughout the time segments booked.
Subject to availability, advertisers preferences will be considered, but cannot be guaranteed.
Spots of longer duration than 30 seconds are pro-rata to the 30 second rate.

			60 seconds	30 seconds	15 seconds
Monday—Friday Saturday Sunday	0600–1000 0700–1400 1000–1500	PRIME (p)	£40.00	£20.00	£14.00
Monday—Friday Saturday Sunday	1000–1400 1600–1900 1400–1900 1500–1900	a	£28.80	£14.40	£10.40
Monday—Friday Saturday Sunday	1400–1600 1900–2200 0600–0700 1900–0200 0700–1000 1900–2200	b	£12.80	£6.40	£4.40
Sunday—Friday	2200–0200	n	£4.00	£2.00	£1.60

whatever they could to plug their new discs and for a time it was customary to include customised lyrics on a special re-recording of the single. Thus Gerry Marsden (of Gerry & The Pacemakers) sent me one 'You won't want to hurry when you listen to Tony Currie ... ' and Simon May (who years later penned the theme music for 'EastEnders') taped another ('Tony Currie is Homeward Bound with you – tune in with me'). A nice idea, but once there were more than a dozen stations around the UK, the practice was dropped – pop groups simply didn't have time to stick around in a studio recording radio station names for hours on end!

Tom Ferrie would be on the air so I'd slip quietly into the studio, through a special soundproof lock with two heavy doors, and once Tom had introduced the next disc and turned the microphone off, we'd have a quick gossip while I arranged my bits and pieces in the studio. Tom would end his stint at 4.30, but at 4.26 he'd play his closing theme ('Love's Theme' by Barry White) from a tape cartridge, and slip out of the chair to let me in. At 4.28 exactly we had a commercial break. Four commercials, each on a separate cartridge; in front of me were six cartridge players, all of them containing a cartridge. As well as the four commercials, there would be Tom's theme and the 261 jingle that we were legally obliged to play at the end of the break.

Once we'd got into commercial number one, Tom's theme tune would be fast wound on to the beginning and taken out of its slot. Then I'd pop in my theme tune ready to play at the press of a button. Meanwhile, I'd also log the exact start time of each commercial in a written log which looked something like this:

Notional Break time: 16.28

Tape no	Advertiser	Duration	Actual time played
352	Arnott's Sale	30"	16:28:07
108	Evening Times	20"	16:28:38
46	Agnew's	40"	16:28:09
226	COI Blood Donor	60"	16:29:40

Which means that at 16.30 and 41 seconds I would fire up the 'Altogether Now' jingle (seven seconds) and at 16.30 and 48 seconds my theme tune would be on the air.

During this sequence, I'd switch my headphones to listen to the output of one of the two turntables, and 'cue up' the first disc. You'd drop the needle as near to the start as you could and then manually wind the record forward or backwards until the needle was at the

The AA Girls (left to right): Marie Lauchlan, Margaret McCulloch and Helen Cree.

precise start. It took a quarter of a revolution of the turntable to get up to the correct speed, so then you'd turn the record back exactly a quarter of a revolution from the beginning. Now it was ready to play.

Once the show had started, and the theme tune was on the air, I had a bank of faders in front of me, with the facility to fade in and out all of the various sound sources: the presenter's microphone, two more on the other side of the studio for guests, and one next door in the news booth. On top of this there were the two turntables. The two faders each connected to a stack of three of the cartridge players, two large reel-to-reel tape players, plus the lines from the AA studio in Erskine and the Independent Radio News studios in London.

Thereafter it was a matter of juggling everything together at the right moment, making sure each item was cued up and ready to play (usually done during the previous item) and using the special talkback intercommunications system that allowed you to talk to the AA reporter at Erskine and the newsreader next door. You'd take a 'level' from each of them before they went on air so that their voices would come out at the same volume as everything else in the programme.

And all the while I was obliged to watch four needles on large meters in front of me, to make sure that the volume was neither too high nor too low; that the stereo signal was 'in phase' (if it went 'out of phase' mono listeners heard nothing); and that both transmitters were still on the air!

Opening night glitches apart, the 'kit' at Radio Clyde was pretty reliable, and technical breakdowns a very rare occurrence, almost always attributable to human error. The 'cart' machines were the only inherent weakness, but at the time we came on air there was nothing else on the market that allowed you to play jingles and commercials with such flexibility. We all took the reliability for granted, and it wasn't until I experienced other television and radio setups that I truly appreciated how well built the studios had been.

Clyde built indeed.

Of course all the while I was broadcasting, I'd be logging the records being played on the 'P as B' copyright form and the commercials as they were played. It was a cardinal sin to forget to play the commercials at the right time (after all they paid our wages!) and it often necessitated juggling the records and doing quick bits of arithmetic on the back of a fag packet to make sure that the commercials would end just as the 5pm news began. (It had to begin at 5pm exactly – not seven seconds later!)

Come the end of the programme, and after yet another quick cup of coffee, time to start thinking about Sunday's classical music programme. I might have a public appearance opening a fête next afternoon, so there wasn't a surplus of time to prepare the Monday night classical programme.

Consequently I'd spend an hour listening to a new classical album, often from the specialist label Nimbus Records. Like, for example, an LP of rare music by Debussy that turned up one week, performed by a former classmate of mine at Ardrossan Academy – a guy by the name of Roy Howat. This obviously had to be included – the music was wonderful, and I could arrange a telephone interview with Roy (who was now working in London) to be recorded on Friday afternoon for inclusion in the programme, which I pre-recorded every Friday night.

After a few phone calls to set up Roy's item, back in to the studio to spend half-an-hour editing Karin Spalter's 'Social and Personal' programme – Karin would sit beside me telling me where to cut the tape – then out for a quick black pudding supper to keep me going!

Evenings were often the time when the music studio was at its busiest. Our resident balance engineer, Pete Shipton, could be found in the throes of capturing the sound of the latest bands on tape and it was always tempting to loll around in the back of the control room awhile and enjoy the buzz. Pete's mixing technique was interesting because he was slightly deaf in one ear, with the consequence that the stereo image of everything he mixed tended to be slightly lop-sided!

At ten o'clock an exchange of pleasantries with Frank Skerret in the canteen, going through his running order for the evening, checking that he had brought all the right records with him, since Frank tended to play discs from his own personal collection. He'd give me a list of whatever albums he needed from the library, which Sandra (or her later replacement Norma Beaton) would have looked out for him, so all I had to do then was nip in to the library and pick up the missing discs and we were ready to go into Studio A. Frank and I would slip quietly in through the sound lock while Brian Ford was on air and a record playing.

Frank placed himself at the 'chat table' opposite the control desk, and when Brian wound up his show, I'd plant myself once again in the 'hot seat' and take over the playing of the 10.28 commercial break. 'Driving' – Frank's show – was very similar to presenting 'Homeward Bound' except I didn't have to speak or think about what to say. Instead as each disc ended, I'd give Frank about 30 seconds' warning and give him a hand cue each time I faded the microphone up for him to speak.

At the end of the show I'd cue in the newsreader for the midnight news bulletin before leaving the studio in the safe hands of Tom Ferrie (yes, we *all* worked long hours!) who hosted Wednesday's midnight to two slot. Then a quick hot chocolate in the canteen (coffee was for keeping me awake) before it was home to bed.

Who said we just came in for 90 minutes in the afternoon … ?

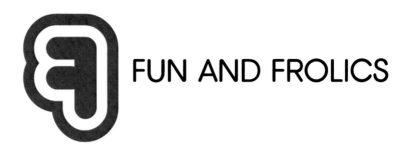

FUN AND FROLICS

When I used to tell people I worked at Radio Clyde, they'd look wistful and say, 'That must be fun'. They never knew the half of it! Life could be one long party. Mind you, sometimes the party could get a tad out of hand. Often on a Friday night. In true Clyde fashion, the late-night show on Friday bore the name 'The Boozy Woogie Rock Party' hosted for three-and-a-half hours (or thereabouts) by Steve Jones and/or whoever else turned up on Friday nights.

It merited its own catchy theme song 'Friday Night is a Beautiful Night', composed and recorded by local songwriter Harry Barry (on RCA Victor, no less), and on a quiet night the show consisted mostly of Steve playing his favourite rock records until he'd finished the bottle of Mateus Rosé that was a permanent adjunct to such occasions. Often visiting pop stars, or other celebs, would turn up and make the gig a genuine party. When that happened, Steve would host the show from the big music Studio B, and the ever-inventive John MacCalman would rustle up an arrangement of coloured lights in the studio to give it a bit more atmosphere. These were usually red, giving the place a palpable air of decadence.

One such evening, the guest (as far as I can remember) was Paul Jones, who has in a previous life been lead singer with Manfred Mann. Twenty or so Clyde family and friends were sitting on the floor of Studio B, and from time to time, Paul Jones (no relation to Steve as he kept telling us) would sing and play the piano. Later in the evening – probably about 1am – Steve decided that because Paul had taken to penning advertising jingles, it might be fun to set him a challenge. Steve challenged him to come up with a brand new jingle for an imaginary product in just half-an-hour. I was roped in to provide the voiceover for the spoof commercial, and not only did we invent a commercial, we also invented a product, which became dafter as the effects of the Mateus Rosé wore on. Much hilarity ensued as we pulled ourselves together sufficiently to broadcast the result on time. I just wish someone had recorded it![3]

Although Radio Clyde nominally closed down at 2am, the music often continued, especially on Fridays. Kenny Page was often left to make the final announcement and play the national anthem. The cart containing it had a habit of vanishing from Studio A, thanks to a technical operator with nationalist sympathies. For artistic rather than political reasons, Kenny would generally substitute a platter of his choice for 'God Save Save The Queen'. On one memorable occasion this turned out to be Mike Oldfield's 'Tubular Bells' – all 50 minutes of it!

Steve's ritual bottle of Mateus Rosé turned out to be the programme's downfall one Friday. Early on a Saturday morning, I was roused by the urgent ringing of the telephone (living closer to the studios than anybody else sometimes had its drawbacks). Tiger Tim was on the line, in a bit of a funk. He had arrived as normal to present the Saturday 'Breakfast Show' only to find Studio A totally wrecked. Most of the previous night's bottle of Mateus appeared to have been spilled over the transmission desk, with the resultant mess fusing all sorts of unlikely electrical circuits together causing nasty loud howling noises on the air. Steve and his chums must have reckoned that it was irreparable and had simply turned off the power and gone home, leaving the mess for somebody else to clear up!

Tiger was now doing his best to present his show from the small Studio C, but since I was the duty technician he had his fingers crossed that I could summon up a miracle to get 'A' working in time for Dave Marshall's 'Children's Choice' at 9am. Yet another fast car into Anderston and it became quite obvious that the control desk was well beyond immediate repair. For a start, there appeared to be a pint of wine floating around in the bottom. Not being a miracle worker myself, I summoned John Lumsden and the rest of his team, and after much head-scratching they decided that the studio had to come out of service for the rest of the weekend for a major cleanup and rebuild.

At this point, Karin Spalter came on the scene to make the point that her afternoon sports programme absolutely depended on the availability of the phone-in gear for all of the football reports – and that gear could *only* be operated from Studio A. More head-scratching resulted in the decision to shift the entire control desk

3 Paul Jones claims to have no memory of this event. Could it have been Mike d'Abo? I don't think so but that Mateus can't half confuse a chap …

Russell Fleming and John Lumsden at work in the Clyde OB unit.

from Studio C into Studio A in order to avoid the wrath of the football fans. Doing this gave us no alternative but to run the station live from Studio B – something which had hitherto never been attempted.

'Not a problem,' reassured engineer Russell Fleming, as he headed off to the engineering bay, armed with a handful of cables and plugs, to 'make it so'.

Frank Skerret was duly enthroned in the totally soundproof music studio and I sat next door in the control room to 'drive' his show as usual. Normally we'd chat to each other all the time the discs were spinning, but in order to do that in Studio B, we had to use an intercom system to talk to each other. As soon as the show had started I checked the 'off-air' switch on the desk which let me listen to a radio receiver to check that what we were playing was actually coming back to us from the transmitter. For no apparent reason, the arrangement in Studio B only allowed me to check that all was well on the 95.1MHz FM transmission. It was, so I made the dangerous assumption that 261 metres medium wave was similarly behaving itself. While the discs played, I proceeded with a narrative of the previous night's events by way of explanation to poor Frank, via the intercom. Doubtless my journalistic inclinations led me to improve on the story somewhat in the telling. Suddenly another of the engineers burst into the control room. 'There's a fire! Somebody's set fire to the rubbish at the bottom of the lift shaft and there's smoke everywhere!'

This was also too good a story to keep to myself and, with suitable added melodrama, I informed Frank that 'now the bloody building's on fire as well!' At this moment our redoubtable telephonist, Ruby MacGregor rushed pale-faced into the room.

'Tony,' she muttered *sotto voce*, 'Tony – there's a problem.'

'Speak up, Ruby!' I responded somewhat *basso profundo*, 'what's up – another fire or is there a dead body in the lift shaft, perhaps?'

I was enjoying this.

'Sssshhh. Everyone'll hear you.'

'Ruby, – what are you on about?'

'Every word you say is going out on medium wave.'

'Ah … '

In his haste to connect the studio to the transmitters, poor Russell – who was most certainly not prone to such gaffes – had plugged the output from the Studio B control room intercom microphone directly to the 261m medium wave transmitter at Dechmont Hill. Listeners had been enjoying my tales of doom all morning without the benefit of hearing Frank's responses. Jimmy Gordon hadn't shared their enjoyment, however, and had frustratingly found the lines permanently engaged as punters rang in on Saturday morning with their record requests. One listener later claimed to have a tape of the entire fiasco. If you're reading this, I'd love a copy.

On Radio Clyde's first anniversary, our friends at Warner Brothers Records gave us a very special birthday present. They allowed us to make a record and pressed thousands of copies for us to give away to our listeners. They'd done the same thing for Capital Radio in London on its anniversary a few months earlier. Andy Park undertook the production of this bizarre single and amassed the troops for yet another all-night recording session in Studio B. We made it all up as we went along (as always!) and by dawn we had taped both sides of the disc.

Given free reign we went mad with the thing – Brian Ford opened it cheekily with a BBC Radio 1 jingle, followed by Brian's words 'Finished. Washed Up. All over. Finished.' The Radio Clyde song followed and at the end we all sang 'Nice one, Jimmy' in tribute to Jimmy Gordon who had made it happen for us all. Clips of programmes, jingles, a weird compilation from Craig Samet of 24 hours condensed into a single minute and Tiger Tim encouraging his teenage phone-in callers to sing along with the jingles were all squeezed on to the seven inches of vinyl. For years afterwards each of us boasted that we were signed to Warner Bros!

Outside broadcasts could be a lot of laughs. A few days after we launched, the *Evening Citizen* invited us to open their annual 'Planning Your Holidays' exhibition at the McLellan Galleries in Sauchiehall Street, with several of our programmes broadcast live from there including 'Homeward Bound'. This was the first chance we'd had to meet the public and we were all astonished at the response as we were constantly mobbed by happy

The birthday disc.

Jennifer Soltysek hands over the infamous coffee percolator.

punters, delighted to put faces to the voices they'd already come to know, and it was a sheer pleasure to meet them. One especially.

Perched up on a stage above the crowd, I was cueing up the next record when I overheard the excited voice of a large bearded guy telling his wife, 'Hey – that's what Tony Currie looks like. Let's go and say hello.' The bloke in question was Billy Connolly!

'Seaside Queen' Jennifer Soltysek, an attractive blond lassie from Dalmuir, presented us with a giant coffee percolator as our fee for the gig. Thereafter the percolator – a particularly sickly colour of green – gathered dust in the corner of our office. We certainly never had enough time to go and fill it up, and none of us could afford to buy packets of ground coffee.

The evidence!

Christmas – a time for enjoyment. Sorry, the last word in that sentence ought to be 'drinking'. In the early years, the management were particularly generous, giving each of us a nice Christmas present. A new radio, portable TV sets, video games ... very nice, too, and one of my Clyde trannies is still doing noble service in the Currie household. The first year, Jimmy decided to give us each a flagon of a special blend of 'Radio Clyde' whisky. This was done at the end of our annual Christmas lunch, held in the station's canteen on 23 December. (Bad move, Jimmy).

Considering there were already bottles of wine *and* whisky at every table and each head of department had invited his staff for a post-lunch piss-up, doling out flagons of whisky did seem a trifle fate-tempting. Most people got tore in at once, though I abstained since I was duty technician and had to operate the panel for Ken Sykora, who was taping his Christmas Eve programme later that afternoon.

Just before five o'clock – by which time the entire building truly was 'altogether stoatin'' – Ken and I sauntered in to the control room of Studio B with his pile of records. Instinctively I threw open the studio microphone fader in order to hear the reassuring tick of the clock that let me know the mic was still working. My ears perked up at what I heard instead.

Groans. Heavy breathing. A familiar voice: 'Oh, you're a gorgeous wee bird. Oh, don't stop. Oh, that's wonderful … '

Of course I did the obvious thing.

I set the studio tape recorder into the 'record' mode.

But here was a dilemma. Entertaining as this live performance of 'Je t'aime' might turn out to be, I did have a two-hour show to record. Expedience got the better of voyeurism and I gently pushed open the studio door (leaving the lights off) and, averting my eyes hollered very loudly,

Ken Sykora choosing music for his show.

'I'll just nip to the loo then before we start our *two-hour recording session*, Ken'.

Ken and I hustled out to watch from behind the cover of the canteen doors. Instantly the couple appeared from behind the studio door, and, believing themselves unobserved, slipped into the commercial production Studio D across the corridor to continue their tryst uninterrupted.[4]

In an unrelated incident, Bill the joiner was found the following morning, upside-down in a store cupboard.

The Altogether Guys and Girls sure knew how to party.

Some months later, the jocks were being wooed by an agent who fancied himself as the godfather of 261. In order to prove how well off the guys could be under his wing, they were invited to a boxing match in Edinburgh with dinner beforehand. Dave Marshall and I declined, since I didn't have any spare time for outside work and Dave needed to sleep some time. But most of the others went along to see how much free drink there might be.

They were certainly not disappointed.

Steve asked politely for a vodka and soda at the start of the evening. There was no sign of it – until he sat down at the dinner table to find two whole bottles at his place, and a crate of soda under the table. 'Jolly generous' thought the Jones boy. Sadly, he never got as far as either the boxing or the second bottle, since bottle number one disappeared in record time, leaving him to sleep off the effects.

---

4 That their antics were being observed that afternoon may now come as something of a shock to the participants when they read this!

Oposite page: Dire warnings from the
MD ... his first 'newsletter'.

Next morning, he crawled off in search of his colleagues. At the
hotel he found 'bodies everywhere' – and a small problem. It was
now ten minutes to nine. The 'Steve Jones Show' was due to begin
at nine o'clock – 40 miles away – and there was clearly no point in
ringing the head of entertainment, since his was one of the bodies ...

A fast car, and lots of apologies, and Steve was on the air only
an hour late – with Dave Marshall filling in for an extra hour. Steve
got hell when he went home to Lolita. Even more so when she
unpacked his case and found an unfamiliar pair of shoes. They
remain unclaimed to this day ...

Working all hours could be murder on the stomach, and late
one Sunday night Steve Jones and I could stand it no longer. Faced
with no nearby open chippies and ravenous hunger, we eyed up the
large padlocked refrigerator in the canteen. With the aid of a few
heavy tools from the workshop, the padlock was quickly prised off
and the Jones Boy and I tucked into a couple of rolls and Lorne
sausage, carefully screwing the hasp back on and returning the
padlock to its former state. We thought we'd got away with it until
Jimmy's first 'Staff Newsletter' came out a few days later.

*'I hesitate to talk in terms of summary dismissal to people whom I
like to think of more as members of the same team than as employees, but
it is a fact that on at least two occasions the refrigerator in the kitchen has
been broken into. I obviously hope that no members of the staff were
involved, but I know you will understand that anyone found either
breaking into the kitchen or guilty of another major misdemeanour
would have to be sacked immediately.'*

So somebody else had also been at the sausages? We took the
hint anyway. And Jimmy had a vending machine installed to
provide sustenance after hours.

Nobody was fired.

Come Christmas, it was natural that we'd want to do a
pantomime. Curiously, however, the initiative for this came not
from the entertainment department but from the newsroom (all
frustrated thespians I reckoned) and for reasons I now can't
remember the task of cobbling something together fell to a team of
me, Karin Spalter and Paul Murricane. Surely we didn't actually
volunteer for this? Over a period of about a fortnight we'd get each
member of the news team to write something silly – a spoof of their
own programme or on-air personality, something topical in
ridiculous rhyme. It had to be recorded in an extraordinarily
piecemeal fashion, taking advantage of rare moments of availability.
Then on 30 December (the panto was going out on Ne'erday) we

3. Finance:

	January	February	March	First Quarter	Year to March, 1974
	£	£	£	£	£
					198,881
Expenditure	47,133	46,327	59,520	152,980	113,822
Revenue	44,160	33,110	36,553	113,822	85,059
Loss	2,973	13,217	22,967	39,158	

Unfortunately, we have as yet not reaped the benefit of the tremendously good audience figures. Sales revenue has been disappointing, but in fairness to our sales staff, both local and national, the whole advertising market has been extremely difficult over the last six months. I am confident that we can expect much better revenue figures over the next quarter, indeed April has already shown a dramatic up-swing.

The figures above exclude heavy capital expenditure totalling over £100,000 While we should break about even for the month of April, it is quite clear that we must not only dramatically increase our revenue, but wherever possible minimise costs if we are to make any in-roads into this heavy deficit.

In general, the building is operating fairly efficiently, and I am sure that no-one is consciously wasting money, but I am equally sure that we could save a bit on our very heavy telephone bills and in unnecessary use of stationery, in particular the expensive photocopying machine. At the moment, we are surviving on what our shareholders have contributed and a bank overdraft of about £80,000, and obviously we want to be paying our way as soon as possible.

4. Staff:

Despite the financial situation, we decided to increase the staff slightly in the last few weeks to ease the undoubted pressures that existed in early January.

Several trade unions have approached our national contractors' association for recognition and the right to recruit staff in independent local radio. Since this is an entirely new industry, there clearly could be teething problems until everything settles down to a pattern. For the moment, the Association of Independent Radio Contractors have recognised A.B.S., A.C.T.T., and the N.U.J., 'though obviously if there were a clear desire on the part of our staff to join another union or to form one we would want to take account of this. I would be glad, therefore, if all members of staff, and indeed contract artistes, would complete and sign the attached form so that I have a picture of the way things might work out in Radio Clyde.

In general, everyone is working hard and enthusiastically, but there has been a tendency in some areas towards poor time-keeping. We do not want to watch the clock too much, but remember, if you are not there your job is not being done, and your job is important, otherwise you would not be with Radio Clyde in the first place. I hesitate to talk in terms of summary dismissal to people whom I like to think of more as members of the same team than as employees, but it is a fact that on at least two occasions the refrigerator in the kitchen has been broken into. I obviously hope that no members of staff were involved, but I know that you will understand that anyone found either breaking into the kitchen or guilty of another major misdemeanor would have to be sacked immediately. Nor can we tolerate a situation where members of staff, without any prior authorisation, open up taxi accounts and charge taxi fares to it. The bills in question have been passed on to the individuals concerned.

RADIO CLYDE LTD.

Registered Office:
House, Blythswood Court,
s Centre, Glasgow G2 7LB.
elephone: 041-204 2555.
Telex No. 779537
ic Address: RADCLYDE
d in Scotland No. 43876.

once a quarter
matters that

its

has
til
r
t
and

th
l

ach day, and

airman), James Gordon (Managing Director), William Brown C.B.E., J Dickson Mabon M.P.,
Kenneth McKellar, A. J. Murray C.A., Sir Iain Stewart, Esmond Wright.

met in the studio to stitch it all together with some vague kind of plot. Very vague. Practically non existent.

One grand wheeze we'd had was to make some spoof ads. But we simply didn't have any time to make them! So Karin suggested we might get everyone together to sing 'Yes, we have no commercials' to the tune of 'Yes, we have no bananas'. This seemed a fun idea until Alex got to hear about it. He stormed into the office in his usual whirlwind way.

'Can't have this, punchy team, can't have this. What if we really don't have any commercials in six months' time, eh? I can see the tabloid headlines now – '261 CREW PREDICTED OWN FATE IN PANTO JIBE'. No, we can't have this. Give the bananas to the DJs, eh? Shake 'em out the trees.'

Undaunted we wrote another song. Playing a lot on 261 at that time was 'Gaudete' by Steeleye Span. We used that tune and wrote a song titled 'Bad News Bores'. A few minutes before the panto was due to air, Karin and I sat in Studio B, ever so slightly tired (I'd hosted the anniversary Hogmanay show the night before) and lacking an ending. Our brains seemed blank. Our spirits low. An idea suddenly came to me.

I rolled the tape, and yelled into the microphone.

'We haven't got an ending!'

'Oh yes we have,' responded the assembled company

'Oh no we haven't'

'Oh yes we jolly well have!'

Ah, there's nothing like a deadline. And our 15 minute pantomime made it!

April 1st was naturally a godsend for the jokers at 261. Pranks abounded, mostly directed at our beloved audience, especially effective if carried out before listeners realised that April Fools' day had actually arrived. Colin MacDonald's Monday night midnight show 'The Folkal Point' was sometimes devoted to exclusives of new releases. One week – on the show billed for 31 March – Colin had been offered an exclusive – the world premiere of Mike Oldfield's 'Hergest Ridge', a work which is perhaps rather a pale shadow of 'Tubular Bells' but which was nonetheless a considerable draw. But not only had Radio Clyde an exclusive on the music.

'If you tune your television set in to the BBC1 channel after

An early publicity postcard for Colin MacDonald's 'Folkal Point' show.

closedown, you'll see the specially produced abstract images that Mike Oldfield has created to go along with the album. We're presenting this as the first TV and radio simulcast of the album. If you've any problems receiving these pictures, ring our helpline on 204 0261 and Tony Currie will be happy to talk you through your difficulties.'

The lines lit up at once. We weren't putting any calls on the air. It was just them – and me. Line 1 ...

'I can't see anything but snow ... '

'Ah, you must be watching on a black and white TV. We're transmitting only a chroma signal and on a mono TV the luminance component will look like a sort of snow.'

' Oh. I see. I'll go round to my brother-in-law's and try it on his telly. He's got colour.'

Line 2 ...

'I cannae see nuthin ... '

'Where are you phoning from?'

'Airdrie – right near Black Hill.'

'Ah, you see we're not transmitting the pictures from Black Hill. They're coming from the Radio Clyde OB caravan parked in Glasgow's West End. So you probably wouldn't be getting a good signal. Do you have an indoor aerial?'

'Aye '

Can you get it up a bit higher?'

'Aye – I'll try standing on the dining table.'

(Sound of furniture being moved)

'How's that?'

'A bit better I think ... ' (Voice slightly distant)

'How's the red?'

'Can't see any.'

'We'll turn it up a bit at our end ... Colin – more red! How does that look?'

'Oh, that's better!'

'You'd better stay up on the table until the end of the programme then, Sir.'

Line 3 ...

'I don't know what it is I'm supposed to be seeing ... ?'

'Well, Mr Oldfield has used a white noise generator and a 4.43 megahertz signal generator to produce a phase-shifted abstract signal.'

'What the hell does that mean?'

'Well, on a domestic TV it means a screen full of crawling dots

… red, green and blue colours, moving at random all the time like little insects or snow falling.'

'Aye – that's right – that's what we've got. (Excitedly) C'm here, mother, we're getting it alright!'

Line 1 …

'It's twenty past one in the morning and I've got dressed again and driven out to my brother-in-law's but neither of us can pick anything up!'

'Where does your brother-in-law live?'

'Kilmarnock.'

'Oh. You should have said. Because this isn't a BBC transmission, the relay station at Darvel won't be receiving the signal and re-broadcasting it. Our transmitter doesn't generate the right codes for the relays to come back on automatically, you see. I'm terribly sorry … '

As a final story in our 2am news, George Montgomery revealed that the 150 callers had all been victims of our April Fool, and that if they wanted to hear the tape recordings of their calls, they should tune in at *5.00am*, a full hour before Dave Marshall was due to come on the air.

Then we put out the lights and quietly sloped off home …

A year later, I was on the air every night until 6am from Studio C. After the 6am news at my handover there would be a bit of banter with Dave, who hosted his show from Studio A. I'd switch control to him from Studio C and crawl off to bed. But not on April Fools' Day.

Dave Marshall is a man of habit. You'd have to be to have coped with the 'Breakfast Show' every day for so long. He always had all his jingles – theme tune, backing tracks, stings,[5] etc – in a neat little plastic carrying case which he would leave on his office desk, along with the 'What's On' information and the running order for the next day's programme before heading home. And we shared the same office, didn't we? … At four in the morning, I had nipped into the office and gently peeled off the sticky label from the cartridge tape containing his theme tune. I then stuck it on to an identical – but blank – cartridge, and replaced this in his box, taking the real

[5] 'Stings' in the radio world have nothing to do with flying insects. They are short and zappy bursts of music of around two or three seconds that are widely used as musical punctuations.

theme tune tape into the studio with me.

At two minutes past six, Dave was, as always, all set and ready with his headphones listening to the return feed from the transmitter so that he could hear my voice handing over to him.

' ... over now to our morning man, Dave Marshall.'

'Our thanks to Tony Currie there for the last four hours. Good morning.'

His finger jabbed at the start button and he slickly faded up his theme tune. Or so he thought. I started my machine at exactly the same moment and faded up the real tape. Up went the lever, up came the music.

Cliff Richard was just one of the stars who popped in to 261. Here he's chatting to Dave Marshall.

To Dave, it all seemed absolutely normal. He'd assumed I'd handed over control by now (I hadn't of course, but the bulb in the light that indicated who had control had burnt out days before) and he'd pressed play and could hear the music. So all in the Marshall garden appeared rosy.

He faded *down* the music to speak over it.

I faded it *up* louder.

'Er. Oh! Good morn ... Good ... what's ... um. ...?'

He faded it *up* again.

I faded it *down*.

Try and put yourself in Dave's place. You're barely awake, and something you have done, as a reflex action, at least a thousand times before, is suddenly functioning in complete reverse. You do not try to understand how. Or why. You merely acknowledge and adapt. So Dave switched to moving the fader *down* to make it louder, and *up* to make it quieter.

'Er, right, something funny with the technicals this morning but here we are and let's just run through the morning.' (Moves fader down. Tune gets louder. Phew. So far so good.)

At this point, I had sneakily rerouted his headphones so that he could hear only what I wanted him to hear, and he was oblivious to the fact that I had very quietly broken into his programme and explained to the listeners exactly what was going on.

So now they were in on the joke as well. In fact, everyone around was hysterical – the newsroom in stitches – but poor Dave ploughed on.

Time for phase two. Time for Dave to read the weather and introduce the first record. This necessitated making the theme tune fade away. So he pushed the fader up.

This time I make it suddenly go very loud indeed!

'Oh! Sorry I ... er ... TONY, WHAT'S GOING ON?'

The immediate and sudden addition of cocks crowing and a World War One gun battle on top of the music had at last suggested to Dave that his shoulder-heaving chum next door was more likely to have an explanation for this extraordinary occurrence than perhaps, say, Mr Mxyzptlk might.

Eventually he forgave me.

Until, that is, the morning he slept in (to my knowledge the only time this ever happened), and I presented the first half-hour of his show mimicking his voice so well that nobody noticed he wasn't there, and he had to endure all this on his car radio as he drove in from Clarkston ...

Dave didn't seem to take many holidays, but one December, Barbara had persuaded him to take a week off, so I was given temporary command of the 'Breakfast Show'.

The week started fine, and it was fun to try out a different slot. A bit like rearranging the furniture. Unfortunately two clouds appeared on my horizon. The first was one of those irritating winter throat infections. The second was the pluggers' parties. In order to ensure maximum play of their new releases, all the major record companies employed young men to use their powers of persuasion on the DJs. This had of course started in London, where skilled 'pluggers' would at one time wheedle BBC, Radio Luxembourg and pirate producers into giving their new waxings a listen.

With the advent of legalised commercial radio, it was inevitable that they'd turn their attentions to the DJs at the new stations, although when there were too many such stations to cope with, the practice died out and the record companies merely mailed envelopes of new singles to jocks at the bigger stations. But in December 1975, Radio Clyde was one of the brightest lamps in the radio firmament, and a veritable posse of promotions men would beat a path to our door. Since there was a plugger for each major label, this had the effect of cancelling out their efforts as we'd play equal amounts of music from all the labels. But they would take us for lunch occasionally and could be relied on to get us 'white labels' of our favourite artists hot off the presses.

And they always gave great Xmas parties ... perhaps too great.

For in this December week, the Polydor party had been arranged for the same night as the Warner Brothers' party. Each label had taken a separate suite at the Albany Hotel (conveniently a few yards across a pedestrian bridge from our studios) and when the double-booking was discovered, a gentlemanly compromise was reached whereby Warners' party would run from 7pm until 11, and Polydor's would begin immediately afterwards. What a sensible idea. Not.

Naturally the entire complement of 261 DJs and producers drank the bar dry courtesy of Warner Brothers, before proceeding to do the same courtesy of Polydor. Around 5am the next morning, one of the lads pointed out to me that my voice has almost completely vanished as I attempted to shout something over the din of the continuing party. Suddenly I was struck with the enormity of my problem; I sobered up instantly and fled to the studios for a large mug of very strong black coffee. Let me tell you something. Coffee does not constitute a cure for laryngitis!

With barely enough of a croak left to speak a single word at a time and with three hours of live radio to fill, a solution suddenly hit me. Quickly I nipped into the voice booth the reporters used for taping their news stories, laced up a reel of tape and recorded a handful of links *one word at a time*.

You're …
Listening …
To …
Radio …
Clyde …
Here's …
Another …
Chart …
Hit …

Then with speed, skill and a fresh razor blade I edited the words together to make complete sentences. In fact, I rather think I had invented voice tracking! Into the studio, play the first link and off we go. Nae problem. A skoosh. Until, that is, Rosemary stomped in with a traffic report.

'Kingston Bridge is blocked by an accident, TC. You'll need to warn drivers.'

Aaargh. Cover blown, I had to grunt the traffic flash in a painful-sounding throaty croak, attracting all the wrong kind of attention from Alex Dickson. I expect he subsequently wrote a memo or six banning breakfast presenters from attending late-night parties …

Nowadays there are stations where you could lose your voice for six months and not a soul would be any the wiser. That's progress, eh?

ALL THROUGH THE NIGHT

From its inception, Radio Clyde matched Radio 2 in transmission hours, opening up just before 6.00 in the morning, and closing down after the 2.00am news bulletin. Apart from Kenny Page's attempts to extend the hours, there were clearly some folk prepared to listen around the clock, as I discovered by somewhat unconventional means.

In the Autumn of 1975, I was taken off 'Homeward Bound'. My choice of music for a peaktime show was, perhaps, a tad eclectic, and anyway it was by now proving difficult to continue with two jobs as my technical workload was beginning to be a strain on top of programme commitments six days a week. So I worked as a technical operator-cum-producer on weekdays, and presented programmes at weekends. This included the Saturday 'Breakfast Show', which generated quite a lot of mail from loyal listeners, and which I enjoyed particularly because it lacked the pressure that Dave's weekday show was under.

One such loyal listener was Christina Mitchell, an elderly lady whose touching devotion to Radio Clyde knew no bounds. She would write to all of us, and sent each of us presents at Christmas and on our birthdays. Most Saturdays I got a letter or card from her asking for a mention. So one Saturday I decide to test my theory that she never slept because her tranny remained tuned in and turned on to 261 at all times.

Because of some European technical rule, we were not allowed to keep our transmitters switched on overnight unless we put out some kind of station identification at regular intervals. This was in case we were causing interference to somebody else's transmissions and they needed to know where the unwanted signals were coming from. John Lumsden had devised a simple method of complying with this legislation. I had recorded an announcement (saying that 'This is Radio Clyde on 261 and 95.1') and this was put on a ten-and-a-half minute 'cart', so that the short announcement would be repeated every ten-and-a-half minutes throughout the night.

Just before 5.20am the announcement came around on the loop once again. Just as it finished, I opened the microphone and said, ' ... so if you're listening, Christina, you've only forty minutes to wait!' Within seconds the studio telephone rang. Christina. She *was* listening!

The success of Radio Clyde in attracting a bigger audience than any other radio station in the area led Jimmy Gordon to make the momentous decision to fill the gap and continue broadcasting for 24 hours a day. 'Like the Windmill Theatre, we'll never close!' he quipped. But who would have the task of presenting the new 2–6am show? For weeks before Hogmanay 1975, a constant stream of new presenters flowed through Andy Park's office. Some were brought in to the studios and Andy frequently requested that I should put them through their paces and pass an opinion on their abilities. With just a few days to go, the announcement still hadn't been made about who the new presenter was.

Bumping into Andy in the corridor, I asked him if he'd made up his mind.

'Sure, we know who's going to take us through the night.'

'Who, Andy?'

'It's you, of course, TC!'

To this day I can't work out whether – in desperation – he came up with this on the spur of the moment, or whether he'd planned to give me the gig all along. The very first all-night show – on Hogmanay – was hosted jointly by Tom Ferrie and Billy Connolly, while I started the new regular show the following Monday night/Tuesday morning.

In the event the 2 till 6 slot turned out to be the best fun I ever had on the wireless. Because the record companies placed a time limit on the amount of commercially-available discs that radio stations could play on any given day, there was a shortage of what the BBC had christened 'needle-time', so 'Through the Night' was only allocated 20 minutes of 'normal' records to play in each four-hour show.

For the rest of the time it had to be specially recorded music; the sort they used on the test card (remember the little girl with the doll?). Instrumentals recorded by anonymous musicians solely for radio and television use are known in the business as 'library music' because it's supplied free by specialist music publishers like KPM Music, Music de Wolfe, Boosey & Hawkes, Southern Music and others. Users pay a fixed fee for playing each track, of course, but it doesn't count as 'needle-time'.

At this point I must confess that I've always had a special passion this kind of upbeat, big pop orchestra stuff (as Andy Park well knew) so I was very much at home with it. Richard Park used to send me up mercilessly for playing a Belgian instrumental outfit called 'The Botticelli Orchestra' on 'Homeward Bound'.

In the wee small hours, I even invented a mythical ensemble. 'The Nitebirds'. In reality, I came across four similar-sounding albums on different libraries, all with the same lineup of vibraphone, drums, bass and flute, and every time I played one of these tracks I'd tell the listeners it was by 'The Nitebirds'. Almost at once, I began getting requests for me to play 'The Nitebirds.' Try that today and you'd have the humourless and artless OFCOM down on you like a ton of bricks for deception.

We also had great bundles of Canadian records, because there's a special rule on Canadian radio that they must play a certain proportion of Canadian-produced material and Clyde bought a barrowload of their discs which didn't count as needle-time. People like The Laurie Bower Singers; Rob McConnell and the Boss Brass; Peter Appleyard; Milan Kymlica. All good stuff and pleasant listening in the wee small hours.

For the rest of the time I would come up with features that might keep the audience amused without playing commercial discs. These included 'The Colour Supplement', a magazine programme starting at 3am and continuing for anything from half-an-hour to a full hour. Amongst the things that crept into this slot were reruns of daytime interview features, sports news, and even a poetry competition.

Surprisingly, there were a good many regular listeners, for it seems that at 3 and 4 in the morning, people concentrate much more on what you're saying than they do at teatime. Often we jocks would discuss the latest letters from our regulars, and we frequently thought how flattered some of them would be if they knew how often their names cropped up in general conversation.

Folk like Gertrude Hill and Sandra Picken, both teenage fans of Cliff Richard. Never slow to send in a request for Cliff's latest single – but after a while they wrote as if we were all old friends, and often I'd find the girls hanging around at the bottom of the studio stairs, waiting to take a photograph or just have a chat. They've probably bored their own children or even grandchildren with these stories by now.

Gordon Dunlop corresponded with every single one of the jocks. An amateur weather forecaster from the south side of the city,

The familiar sleeve of Canadian Talent Library discs.

his local predictions always seemed a damn sight more accurate than those of the Meteorological Office who supplied our official forecasts. When the Met office went on a 24-hour strike, I persuaded Alex to allow Gordon to provide Clyde's forecasts. I swear it's the only time they were 100% right.

One night we had a call from a maternity ward – a lady was in labour and listening to the programme for some diversion. When the baby was eventually born, they named him Tony! Letters alone don't make a show, of course, and my brain was constantly taxed for new ideas. During a warm spell I had the notion to try a cookery spot, and during the evening I made some ice-cream in my kitchen at home, recording a commentary as I went along. Then with a bit of music added here and there to cover the boring bits like mixing and beating, it all turned into 'Currie's Kitchen' which became a regular weekly feature.

I constantly expected it to be taken off – especially after I gave the wrong cooking time for Steak and Kidney Pie …

But after six weeks I reckoned the idea had probably outlived its usefulness and it came to an end. Next day, I was summoned to Jimmy Gordon's office and told – in no uncertain terms – to reinstate 'Currie's Kitchen' immediately! It appeared that its popularity was somewhat greater than I had anticipated.

Thus every Monday in the late afternoon, Karin had to give our kitchen a wide berth and, apron neatly tied around my waist – I wished it was television – I'd set up the elaborate recording apparatus. Cooking is great fun, but having to set up a studio microphone on a boom arm in just the right bit of the kitchen to be able to have your hands free and yet always be properly heard requires some skill on the part of both the sound technician and the presenter (me, obviously). Avoiding dipping a £235 microphone or a £1,000 tape recorder in flour, egg, golden syrup or breadcrumbs was also desirable.

Cooking over, it was straight into the studio (built into the sun parlour of our Pollokshields flat) to time all the lengthy bits with a stopwatch. This was Real Time Recipes. Chopping an onion – 1 min 43 seconds. Whipping egg-whites – 3 min 49 seconds. Then into the record library to consult the catalogues of the specialist background music companies. Never mind the tune, feel the width.

Suitable tunes would be identified and played to see how appropriate they were. Then they'd be mixed into the master recording at the right places, making it sound as if the whole thing was effortless! In total, the production of a 20-minute 'Currie's

Kitchen' would eat up about three hours of my Monday.

Ultimately the feature lasted 13 weeks and years afterwards people still write to me to ask for my ice cream recipe. It's really simple.

Currie's Kitchen – ice cream
You'll need:
4 large eggs
3oz/85g icing sugar
10fl oz/300ml double cream
2 drops vanilla essence

First, clear out an adequate space in the freezer. Get out three mixing bowls (I said three and I mean three) and a plastic box or dish sufficient to take the finished product. I always use a soufflé dish which is just the right size. But you're not getting mine so you'll just have to find your own.

Now you separate the yolks and put them aside. Whisk the whites until they're stiff enough to make meringues.

In bowl number three, whip the cream until just right for filling the meringues we're not making.

Back to bowl number one (stick numbers on them if you're confused) where we add the vanilla essence to the yolks and stir together until nicely amalgamated. (Look it up if you don't understand. I'm trying to cook, here.)

Now we introduce the yolks to the whipped cream (yolks – meet the cream, cream – these are the egg yolks) and whip some more. Add the sugar and whip a bit more.

Fold in the egg whites and whisk briefly to disperse any white flecks. Now transfer to the final dish and freeze for at the least three hours but preferably overnight.

It requires no attention during freezing and comes out at the right consistency to serve it scooped into a cone if you like. And with a chocolate flake bar too if you want to be really hedonistic. It came as a real shock when I joined the BBC some 20 years later to find that one of my colleagues there had, as a teenager, taped the entire series while his parents thought he was asleep!

Food gained disproportionate importance during the night-shift, as anyone who's worked late hours will know. Because we overnight presenters had to turn day into night we all fancied a good feed around four in the morning. This created something of a problem for our hard-pressed canteen staff (Big May had by now

GLASGOW
September 16-29 1974

radio
listening

RADIO AUDIENCE MEASUREMENT LIMITED, 76/86 STRAND, LONDON WC2R 0DZ

SPECIALLY PREPARED FOR
Radio Clyde

THE RATINGS

Radio Clyde's first proper ratings were published in September of 1974 when Radio Audience Measurement Ltd did a thorough survey. The results would double the size of this little book, but some figures extracted from these ratings are interesting.

Radio Clyde's weekly reach was 995,000 representing 65% of all adults in the Glasgow area. Each listener spent an average of 13.1 hours a week with their ears glued to 261.

Peak weekday audience was between 8 and 8.30am when an average of some 189,000 adults (15+) were tuned to Dave Marshall's 'Breakfast Show'.

'Homeward Bound' (with Richard Park) peaked at 4.30pm with 98,000 listening grown-ups while my own effort, 'Homeward Bound part 2' at 5.50pm pulled in 74,000. Steve Jones attracted an average of 168,000 in the first half-hour of his show, Richard Park 147,000 and Maggie Cockburn and Tom Ferrie 97,000.

At the weekend, the top spot was 10am on Saturday - Dave Marshall's 'Children's Choice' - with 242,000. The lowest measured audience of the week was 6,000 between 1.30 and 2am on Sunday night towards the end of Jim Waugh's jazz programme.

While Dave Marshall was coaxing his 189,000 listeners to leave the tuning dial alone, 136,000 preferred Noel Edmonds on Radio 1; 47,000 chose Wogan on Radio 2; 4,000 liked to be woken up with classical music on Radio 3, and 81,000 tuned to BBC Radio Scotland's 'Good Morning Scotland'. In fact at almost any time of the day, Radio Clyde had the largest percentage of the available audience, except for Sundays when at lunchtime, Radio Clyde 'Worldwide' lost out to Radio 1 for its entire duration, and Alan Freeman's ' Pick of the Pops' won 204,000 listeners to Clyde's 80,000.

been replaced by the very competent Fiona) who clearly didn't fancy hanging around all night in case Iain Anderson took a notion for egg and chips at half-past-three on a Monday morning. And I couldn't be making ice cream every day, you know.

The solution was to provide a small freezer and one of these newfangled microwave cookers. Brilliant! The canteen staff simply put away a couple of the lunchtime dishes and quick-froze them for the night crew. We all appreciated it greatly, even if it was a tad inconvenient to try and enjoy a nice dinner whilst presenting a show. I then hit on the idea of pre-recording half-an-hour every night. 'The Solid Music Section'. This I'd do in my own radio studio at home, and bring the tape in without anybody knowing. So every morning while the half-hour from 4.15 was on tape, I would tuck in to my dinner with impunity!

Sometimes however the overnight shift had its own special hazards – the afore-mentioned Mike Russell being only one of those! One night a phone call came in to the ex-directory engineering number. The voice on the other end claimed to represent a terrorist organisation and warned that there was a bomb in our building. I was highly sceptical, but the security man uncharacteristically leapt into action and called in the police, who insisted that the building has to be evacuated at once. Naturally, we had a special procedure to deal with such a crisis. A key was held in the engineering workshop. This – when inserted in an appropriate keyhole – switched the transmitters to a feed from our outside broadcast caravan, which was parked underneath the building. (Why anybody thought it safer to be right underneath the building than on the third floor during an explosion defeated me, but there you go.) The plan was that – in the event of an emergency – the DJ would rush into engineering, put the key into the switch, zip down to the caravan and continue their programme from the duplicate set of equipment it contained.

So I put on Richard Harris' record of 'Macarthur Park' (7 min 45 seconds), and rushed through to engineering.

I found the key, alright. The only problem was there wasn't a keyhole anywhere to be seen. Out of curiosity I ran down the stairs three at a time and investigated the contents of the caravan.

Entirely empty. No equipment there at all.

I headed for the car park where the music production team – who had been working on a late-night recording session – were decamped and happily tucking into a bottle of brandy that producer Dave Murricane had thoughtfully provided. All very pleasant, but after a couple of minutes I decided to take my chances and return to the building. After all, the record was about to finish! Reluctantly, the police let me back in. No, there was no bomb. Excitement over.

The 'Colour Supplement' had the same propensity as Topsy, growing longer and more interesting as the weeks went on. Karin and I were invited to the celebration of '101 years of British Comics' in London; three days of meeting and interviewing some of the wonderful characters who had written or drawn comic strips like 'Rupert the Bear', 'The Bash Street Kids', 'Marvelman' or 'Dan Dare' that reaped rich aural rewards. In fact we came back with so much material that each of us produced our own hour-long documentary on the subject; Karin's went out in a 7pm evening slot and mine of course became a 'Colour Supplement' extra.

Such was the excitement and energy of the comic artists, few of whom had ever met before this extraordinary occasion, that we became friends with several, and perhaps one of the greatest honours I ever received when at Clyde was to be made an honorary member of the SSI – The Society of Strip Illustrators, an honour substantiated many years later when I genuinely wrote and drew a handful of cartoon strips, one for the ITC House magazine, and the rest for the BBC's in-house journal, *Ariel*.

On my very last night on a full-time contract at Radio Clyde – in the Spring of 1976 – I invited a number of chums to join me in the studio for the final edition of 'Through the Night'. They included long-standing friend Bob Christie, who was by then a BBC announcer. It seemed a jolly jape to invite him to read the weather. He also appreciated the jollity of this and read the forecast in a heavily-disguised voice under the *nom de plume* Christie Robertson.

Yeah, right.

Next morning one of his colleagues passed him in the corridor of Broadcasting House.

'Heard you reading the weather on Radio Clyde last night, Bob. What on earth was wrong with your voice?'

9 A CONSTELLATION OF STARS

Radio Clyde was a magnet to every passing pop, film or TV star, probably because until its inception there had been few outlets in Scotland where any of them could plug their latest record/film/series/book or whatever. The BBC had renamed what was the Scottish version of Radio 4 'Radio Scotland' on the day of our launch, but even so a large proportion of its output was fed from down south, leaving just a few hours each day for Scottish-produced material. In contrast, here we were at Anderston Cross trying to fill 24 hours each and every day.

Naturally it was a thrill when well-known personalities dropped in and often we'd persuade them to do more than they had bargained for. Julie Felix dropped by to promote a new record and found herself installed in Studio B recording jingles for each of the jocks! Lulu dropped in for ten minutes and felt so much at home that she stayed to sample the delights of Big May's chips in our canteen, her accent becoming thicker by the minute! Canadian-born Avengers girl Linda Thorson guested on 'Homeward Bound'. She was playing Titania in a new production of A Midsummer Night's Dream and extended an invitation to see the play. This created a slight problem, as the show was due to finish at exactly the same moment that the curtain was due to rise. Undaunted, I taped the last 45 minutes and bribed one of the technicians to 'mind' the tape machine for me while I sneaked off to the theatre!

At this point you might be wondering just how much of 'live' radio was actually a recording. Only rarely did the daytime jocks risk taping their shows, since we had to be prepared for last-minute traffic news, weather flashes, etc. But many of the evening shows and practically everything at the weekend from about 4pm onwards was on tape. One of the technical operators – quite often me – sat in the studio at the weekend and played the tapes, providing a live voice in case of emergency.

One of the nicest people to pass through our studios was the legendary American singer Neil Sedaka. We organised a special

Avengers girl Tara King - alias Linda Thorson.

90

'Homeward Bound' competition with tickets to his show and a chance to meet the man himself as prizes. True to his word, he came on the programme as a guest, chatting to the prizewinners and putting them at ease.

Disappointingly, I had a ghastly bout of flu and although I somehow got through the show I really couldn't face going to the concert afterwards (something which I have always regretted). 'Never mind,' said Neil, 'we'll be thinking of you.' A week later, my office phone rang.

'Hi, Tony! It's Neil Sedaka. I'm still on tour, and I'm calling from Japan – I just rang to see if your flu was better!'

What a star!

Not all of the stars were quite as wonderful,

Sedaka is back!

though. Slade appeared on Richard Park's 'Lunchtime Show', and demanded a huge plate of Big May's chips, a bottle of tomato ketchup and a loaf of bread so that they could construct chip butties, which they then proceeded to hurl at each other. It was at their concert later that day that the editor of *19* (the teenage magazine) showed me how lightly masticated paper tissues make a most effective set of ear-plugs ...

The Bay City Rollers were smuggled in on a Sunday afternoon to tape an interview. No matter which of them Brian Ford threw a question at, it was their sleazy manager, who responded with,

'What Woody is trying to say is ... '

'Alan will tell you that ... '

'Aye, Eric's favourite food is ... '

'Derek likes tall girls ... '

'Sure, as Leslie will tell ye ... '

None of the boys seemed capable of speech. Whether any of them could actually string more than two words together, we never found out. The masticated tissues trick came in handy at their gig as well ...

Pink Floyd sent crimson limousines to ferry us all to their concert in Edinburgh, and Steve Jones and I fell asleep on the way home in the back of a sheepskin–lined palace on wheels.

Sometimes we would have as little idea about who the guests who appeared on our shows were as the listeners. One Saturday lunchtime Annie Wood slipped conspiratorially into the studio to tell me that a group had just turned up at reception clutching their

The only thing Tam Paton didn't do was sing ...

latest album. 'You'd better interview them. They've come all the way from England – it'd be rude to send them away!' So in trooped Big John's Rock 'n' Roll Circus.

Who?

Big John turned out to be songwriter John Goodison who had teamed up with Phil Wainman to form a new band – previously having led another outfit called Blackwater Junction, with arranger Colin Frechter. (His was the only name I found in any way familiar. I possessed an utterly dire EP of TV Themes he'd recorded for a low-budget label many years before.)

That was about all I could glean from a singularly ineffectual interview. Whether they believed DJs to be mindreaders, able to know what questions to ask when bereft of even a single-page press release, I know not. It's a pity they hadn't alerted me beforehand to the fact that Wainman and Goodison wrote songs for The Bay City Rollers, and Colin Frechter was the Rollers' musical director. We might have had more to talk about.

I'm afraid the Rock 'n' Roll Circus album never got played again, and it still sits – 24 years on – in a virgin state on the shelves of my record library at home. Its moment on Ebay cannot be far away.

Big John's Rock 'n Roll Circus. No reasonable offer refused.

In March 1975, we were visited by one Reg Dwight. Elton John, to his fans. He was doing a tour of the UK, and to coincide with each of his concerts he'd pop in to the local radio station en route for a guest appearance. His publicity people thoughtfully sent us a list of the 20 discs he wanted to play during his hour on the air. The format remained the same wherever he went.

It was truly deathly.

'Hi there, this is Fred Bloggs with my very, very special guest, my verrry good friend, Elton John, here on the Fred Bloggs Show on Radio Lower Piddlington. Hi there, Elt! What groovy sounds have you got for us here on the Fred Bloggs Show?'

Elton would be placed at a chat table, with the ensuing broadcast a masterpiece of non-communication between egotistical host and bored superstar.

Andy Park called me into his office.

'He's coming on Tam Ferrie's show this afternoon. We can't let him suffer, wee pal. I want you to produce the thing, give it a bit of life. Listen to his gig on Radio Forth this morning and see if you get any inspiration.' Now I knew that Tom Ferrie would never let Elton John sound like a prat, so we were already ahead of the game. His Radio Forth gig didn't sound much different from the above routine. But an idea began to form in my head …

Promptly at a quarter to two, Elton John arrived, a small energetic man dressed very smartly in a green velvet jacket. We were introduced, and I escorted him along the corridor to Studio A. Inside, I pointed to the chair he was to sit in.

Tony Currie, Elton John, Sandy Jardine, Tom Ferrie.

'But … but that's the presenter's chair!' Too right Elton, you're the man. Tom sat at the chat table, and played the role of guest on the 'Elton John Show' but it was firmly Elton's gig.

'But I can't operate the panel!' I told him he had 15 minutes to learn …

The show opened with me guiding his hands on the controls. But he very quickly picked up the techniques of cueing records, tapes, cartridges and microphones. After 20 odd years in the music business it would have been strange if he hadn't some kind of affinity with this kind of equipment.

As his confidence grew, he relaxed into the show, becoming ever more daring. He read the traffic news, played the commercials and even signed the commercial log.

'This is fantastic. What else can I do?'

I mentioned that he might like to invite his own choice of guests on to the show.

'How do I get them here?'

'You just open the mike and ask them to come in. *Everybody* listens to 261.'

He summoned Billy Connolly. The Big Yin turned up breathless at Anderston Cross within minutes. Likewise some of Elton's Scottish football heroes, like Sandy Jardine. (The fact that all of them were Tom Ferrie's pals might have helped a bit but we never said …)

The 'hour' became two. Then two-and-a-half.

Now it was nearly time for 'Homeward Bound'. Ironically I was due to share my show that night with Kiki Dee (she and Elton having reached number one with their duet 'Don't Go Breaking my Heart'). Twice previously, fate had conspired to prevent her reaching Glasgow as my guest and we were running a funny trailer of the 'will she, won't she turn up?' variety.

Kiki – a charming and vivacious lady with a wicked sense of humour – had already nearly got me fired. I'd interviewed her in her busy dressing room at the Apollo in Glasgow not long after we first went on the air. As the place was very noisy, Kiki had suggested recording the interview in the loo. 'I've got an idea', she said. 'When we finish I'll flush the loo – bound to get a laugh, eh?'

We ended the interview, Kiki said 'Can I stand up, now?' and flushed the loo. It was really funny at the time but when I played it on air the next day, Alex Dickson had one of his annoying sense-of-humour failures and stormed into the studio, threatening me with a P45 for the crime of indulging in bad-taste jokes. Fortunately, Andy saw the funny side and got Alex off my back.

Back to the Elton John Show. Around a quarter-to-four, Kiki rang me from Manchester airport. Abject apologies, but the plane was fogbound and there's no way she would make it to Glasgow.

I made an instant decision.

'Sorry, Elton, but Kiki can't make it for the show. Why don't you stay and host Homeward Bound as well?'

Of course he did. By now he wanted to read the news, play the jingles – in short, he'd become one of the 'Altogether Guys'. In the end he hosted a four-hour airshift. It was brilliant.

'Now I'd like to do something for all of you', he said as he hung up his headphones. He ordered a case of champagne to be brought over from his hotel, we all trooped along to Studio B, he settled down at the piano and – instant party! He played and sang for the entire Clyde team for the whole of a most unforgettable evening. All of this stood him in good stead, incidentally, because some months later he was given his own gig as a jock on BBC Radio 1!

It would be nice to think that we were always as nice to the stars as Elton John was to us, but one lunchtime, I made a right prat of myself. We all engaged in a bit of banter with each other from time to time – like any family, teasing was part of the routine. I dropped in to Studio A during Richard Park's show. I walked straight in, unaware that there were three people sitting round the chat table.

'So what do you think of the show today, TC?' quoth the good doctor.

'The usual crap. How do you get away with such rubbish? Nobody's listening, and that stuff you're playing now is pure garbage. Keech. Melt it down for ashtrays!'

The record on the turntable was 'Take Good Care of Yourself' by The Three Degrees. The three figures around the chat table were The Three Degrees. Oh, shit! The bright atmosphere that Richard had so carefully created in the studio died stone dead. Three Degrees – convinced that the whole gig was a bummer – became totally deflated. The energy drained instantly out of the proceedings. Disaster.

And all down to me and my big mouth.

I resolved never to make flippant remarks to anybody when they're on the air. Sorry, girls. Sorry, Richard ...

My personal musical heroes were rather different to those of my colleagues. Number one on the list was – and still is pianist/composer/arranger Johnny Pearson, whose recording of 'Cast Your Fate To The Wind' which he arranged, conducted and played for Sounds Orchestral remains one of my all-time favourites. I have all his albums.

It was therefore a wonderful joy to be a Clyde DJ and able to arrange to meet my hero in a recording studio in London to talk with him about his life and his music for the 'Hear me Talkin'' series in which each of us would take turns to talk to those we were musically most at ease with. (I had already done a show with Middle of the Road whose greatest hits included 'Chirpy Chirpy Cheep Cheep' and most of whom were from Glasgow).

Composer and pianist Johnny Pearson.

Johnny Pearson turned out to be utterly captivating and after an hour's interview he invited me to be his guest on the set of 'Top of the Pops' for which he was Musical Director.

We remained friends after that and long after the Radio Clyde days, I found myself producing and releasing one of his records on my own label. All thanks to 261.

Another musical hero is Herb Alpert, the American trumpet player, one time leader of the Tijuana Brass and at that time joint owner of A&M Records (the letters stand for Alpert & Moss) the biggest independent label in the world. I was overjoyed when A&M told me that Herb was flying in to Edinburgh for a concert and would be happy for me to interview him there.

Off to the capital city at lunchtime and a bit of a wait in the VIP lounge where there was also a BBC Television news film crew. They asked if they could 'do' him first as they have to get back and process the film for that evening's 'Reporting Scotland'. Fine by me. The interviewer was Kenneth Roy, not a man who ever claimed to be a great musical authority.

Herb was wheeled in with a pretty lady in tow. Ken did his best but Herb – who is not only a very shy man but was also only just recovering from a breakdown – gave not a lot in response to the stock questions about how he felt to be in Edinburgh and what he knew about bullfighting. They ended up with about 50 seconds.

As the film crew took down the lights and prepared to whiz back to Glasgow, Ken whispered in my ear, 'I don't fancy your chances, Tony. He's a dour bugger. You'll get a minute if you're lucky. Good luck.'

As soon as they'd left, I sat down quietly with Herb – still sitting beside the silent, smiling lady – and turned on my tape recorder.

'Well, with me now are two very charming people, Herb Alpert and Lani Hall. Welcome to Scotland … '

A huge smile spread over Alpert's face as I mentioned the lady's name. Lani Hall was the enchanting and extraordinarily talented former lead singer with Sergio Mendes and Brazil '66, and the two of them were what Hollywood used to call 'an item' – indeed they were married soon afterwards. She had brought him through two years of personal trauma and persuaded him first to record again and then to tour. He dedicates every album to her with his love.

His pride was obvious when I began to talk about them together rather than solely about him. Within moments he was relaxed and I ended up with a good seven minutes of interview. It was warm radio. It was the Radio Clyde way of doing things. And there is no substitute for knowing the score before you begin.

Herb Alpert and the author in LA, 2007.

I was thrilled some thirty years later when BBC Radio 2 wanted to make the Herb Alpert Story – the only interviewer he was prepared to talk to was me.

10 CLYDE GUIDE

As Radio Clyde grew into maturity, changes to the original team were inevitable. My place at teatime was ably taken over by Brian Ford, and after my spell as first host of 'Through the Night' I was lured by the bright lights of Scottish Television, leaving the station in April 1976. Like so many, though, it wasn't long before I was back at Anderston Cross – at first I was invited to host the Sunday night/Monday morning edition of 'Through the Night' for a spell, taking over from Iain Anderson whose workload had become impossible.

Then the 'Popular Classics' series – which had been taken away from me with such haste one weekend that I'd trailed the following week's show without realising that it wasn't going to happen – was happily restored under a snappy new name, thought up by Jimmy Gordon – 'Nothing But The Best'.

I was one of the few of the original team to jump ship early, although my first night colleague and best man, Paul Murricane, left on the same day as me. By the autumn of 1978, most of the original team were still to be heard in their original slots – although clearly 'Homeward Bound' was destined always to be the fly in the ointment, since Brian Ford had by now also been replaced, this time by Dougie Donnelly.

Dougie had already made a name for himself in the night-time slot, and his gentle manner and quiet charm made him a natural for daytime.

It was now that the ever-innovative Jimmy Gordon sprang another surprise. For a long time, there had been a high–level argument raging over the question of radio listings. Television listings were for many decades a carefully guarded commodity, with the BBC owning the copyright in its programme schedules and ITV likewise. *Radio Times* enjoyed the biggest circulation of any magazine in the world by virtue of being the only publication with

Dougie Donnelly.

the right to print the BBC programmes a week in advance; *TV Times* made its profit on the similar basis that it, and only it could print the ITV programmes for the week ahead.

These monopoly positions meant that, in order to know what could be seen on all three TV channels, you needed both magazines. A position of which many were critical and indeed one which was not sustainable for much longer.

In 1978 few daily newspapers were prepared to carry the listings for the Independent Local Radio stations' programmes. Many attempts to persuade *TV Times* to carry the Radio Clyde programmes in its Central Scotland edition had failed. So, if you were lucky, the entire day's schedule would be reproduced in your average newspaper in this way:

R. Clyde (*261, 95.1*) 6 – Dave Marshall, 9 – Steve Jones, 12 – Richard Park, 2 – Tom Ferrie, 4 – Dougie Donnelly, 5.30 – News, Clydewide, 7 – Noticeboard, 8 – Tiger Tim, 10 – News, 10.5 – Authors, 10.30 – Iain Anderson, 12 – Colin MacDonald, 2 – Jim Waugh.

Contrast this with the amount of space *Radio Times* devoted at that time to a single radio programme with a 15-minute running time ...

10.45 Morning Story
A Touching Memory by Daphne Fae Glazer
Read by Sonia Elliman.
'As she sipped her mug of tea and listened to the spluttering of the gas fire, she imagined him sitting in the house next door. Odd, she couldn't evenremember what he was called. That must be a trick of the unconscious.'
Producer Gillian Hush

Jimmy Gordon had boldly decided to do something about this. The 'something' was *Clyde Guide*. Radio Clyde's answer to *Radio Times*.

One of the things that pirate station Radio Scotland had realised early on was that the best way to market your radio station was in print, and by having your own publication you could punt your DJs and station in a variety of subtle, and not – so – subtle ways.

Thus, by putting Lulu on the cover of the very first edition of *242 Showbeat*, Radio Scotland had indulged in a neat bit of 'success–by–association' even though Lulu neither worked for them, nor appeared on their station (except when they played her records, of course).

The editorial team of *Clyde Guide* consisted of editor Roddy Forsyth (a local newspaperman), production man Bill Fitzgerald, writer/reporters John Fitzpatrick, Morna Chambers and Billy Sloan with photographer Jack Middleton. Robert Serafin led an advertising sales team of three and Bob McWilliam looked after circulation. There were two office assistants while Alan White, Neil Davies and Cliff Hanley Jr took care of the paper's graphics and art. Russell Gilchrist was general manager of this team of 17 who were based not in Anderston Cross, rather oddly, but in a first-floor office in the middle of Royal Exchange Square. There must have been a good reason at the time.

Issue no. 1 hit the streets of Glasgow on 28th September 1978 – exactly 55 years to the day after *The Radio Times* made its debut as the world's first broadcast listings magazine.

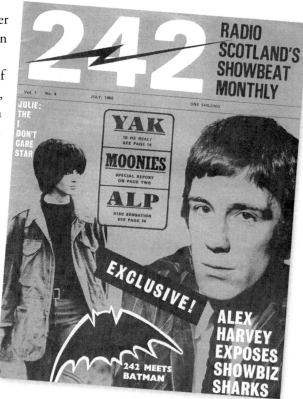

The paper was a broadsheet (unusual for a listings magazine) and was aimed at the *NME* or *Melody Maker* end of the market. Debbie Harry (lead singer of Blondie) had the honour of being the first cover star and the front page was awash with little lumps of text – inviting you to enter competitions, follow the soccer coaching series; or check out some of the regular columnists.

There was naturally a generous smattering of programme-related feature material. A page three feature story told tales of Tiger Tim's recent holiday in Italy alongside items of gossip about other DJs. Frank Skerret was given his own column; Paul Coia penned the film review; the 'Interact' arts team were credited as compilers of the theatre listings (whether that was true or not I never found out); Alex Dickson inevitably had a book review page; Sheila Duffy's recipes for the week were revealed; Colin MacDonald wrote about folk music; Jim Waugh presided over a jazz column and of course Bill Black contributed to the country music section.

Although the programmes themselves hardly changed much week on week, the paper had a centrefold with the weekly listings. A novel idea, as it was printed at right angles to the rest of the text in the paper, and was designed as a pullout to be pinned to the wall, poster-style.

Morna Chambers making the most of the Radio Clyde festival in the summer of '79.

For each day of the week there was a paragraph or two about one individual programme selected from the day's output, and information about programmes themselves. Steve Jones, for example, was granted a somewhat more detailed billing than he used to receive:

9.05 The Steve Jones Mid-morning Show

Steve's daily variety show in three acts, with maximum music, Recipe Time and Dial-a-Dedication in the first hour, followed by the chance to collect cash prizes in the middle hour with the Money Game and heading towards 12 noon with Choose-a-Choon, Country Corner and Problem Time.

Naturally, *Clyde Guide* was stuffed with pictures, including new ones of the DJs. In fact, considering the tiny budget that the paper had, and the minimal resources, the amount of genuine programme-related material was very substantial in the 28-page launch number. The launch itself was something of a low-key affair, with a lunchtime drinks party in a local nightclub. A couple of speeches, a few sausage rolls and everybody trotted home with half a dozen copies clutched to their bosoms.

Over the coming weeks, the eye-catching appeal of the cover varied somewhat. Overloaded with coloured blobs, flashes, headlines, it became like a parody of *The Sun*. Cliff Richard and Joan Armatrading shared cover number two, while an arresting photograph of Brian Ford sitting in a rubbish dump adorned number three, and 'Rochdale Cowboy' Mike Harding appeared in the fourth.

It was the cover of issue five which gave *Clyde Guide* its edge – a large picture of Steve Jones hiding behind a 'Sorry You're Leaving' card, revealing that both the Jones Boy and Tom Ferrie were the next pair to jump ship and leave the Radio Clyde family. Steve was going back to London to become a TV star, hosting 'The Pyramid Game' for LWT, and Tom Ferrie was headed for Queen Margaret Drive to host his own daily show as part of the BBC's re–vamped

The historic first issue of *Clyde Guide*.

Radio Scotland. Steve's replacement was to be Jeff Cooper, and the amiable Bill Smith took over Tom's show.

It was typical of the Clyde family that news of both these departures was presented in accurate detail in the paper, with no fudging about where they were going to. Clyde clearly saw it as good news that 'their' boys were about to make it big somewhere else, and celebrated their good fortune along with them.

As Hogmanay approached, and Radio Clyde celebrated its fifth anniversary, a new feature was added to the paper – a weekly cartoon strip following the adventures of a new Glasgow superhero – 'DNA Man'. The series, written and drawn by Cliff Hanley Jr (the son of 'Heckle Hanley'), was set in the year 2000.

What rather set it aside from other strips was the fact that it was totally and utterly incomprehensible. Nobody had a clue what it was about. But it adorned the back page each week, and the artwork was great ...

The circulation, however, was not.

Part of the problem was that the paper was printed in Dunfermline (on the east coast) and so, circulation manager Bob McWilliam – coincidentally yet another pal from bedroom radio days in Ardrossan – had to whiz through in an estate car and grab the entire print run, then ferry it through to Glasgow and start getting the copies into the newsagent's hands.

Not enough were selling. Pretty soon advertisers realised this and revenue diminished. *Clyde Guide* thinned down to 20 pages. The paper received an overhaul in February 1979, at which time the editorial team consisted of Loudon Temple as news editor, John Fitzpatrick as sub, and Morna, Billy and Joy Rattray as writers. Gone was the cluttered front page, instead the first new-look cover had a Cliff Hanley Jr

A load of rubbish. And Brian Ford!

Steve Jones, Jimmy Gordon and Jeff Cooper as Steve bids farewell to 261 and hands his show over to Jeff.

'Spider Man' creator Stan Lee checking out the 'DNA Man' strip.

The first 'DNA Man' strip.

sketch of Lauren Bacall, Alex Dickson's guest in his weekly 'Authors' slot.

The programme billings were expanded by an extra page, and the graphic design improved. Most of the advertising appeared to be for local restaurants, hotels, pubs and cinemas. By May, Morna Chambers had moved over to work at Radio Clyde itself as a journalist, and I was offered the job of billings editor, looking after the programme pages, writing the billings and researching or commissioning the photos to illustrate them.

What qualifications had I for this task? A lifetime passion for programme guides. I learned to read using *Radio Times* and had built up (from the age of 11) a formidable collection of thousands of programme magazines from around the world. Indeed, I had stashed away copies of *Radio Times* going back to the first issue in 1923 and as a result of many years studying the different ways in which programme information had been translated to type, I probably had as good an understanding of this specialised area as anybody else locally. I readily agreed to work for the paper one day a week.

The first issue with my efforts as billings editor came out on 26 May in issue number 34 and I was thrilled to bits to see the results of my efforts in print.

But I reckoned the programme pages were not right yet and pleaded for the opportunity to go for a complete redesign in the autumn. This was agreed, but I was acutely aware that advertising sales were constantly on the downward slide. The following week I noticed a full-page advertisement for Audio-Technica record player cartridges that included a reply coupon. The reference number on the coupon was DI5. This aroused my suspicions.

When an advertiser includes any kind of reader response – a coupon, a number to phone, an address to write to – he usually gives it a code so that he can tell which newspaper or magazine the reader is responding to. He will see that if he advertised in, say, both *Radio Times* and *TV Times*, and gets 600 coupons back with the code RT1 and only 50 with the code TVT1, his money was better spent on the BBC periodical.

Clearly such ads in *Clyde Guide* would have shown a coupon code of CG1 (or something similar). I also knew that DI5 stood for *Disco International.* A brief conversation with the sales department confirmed my worst fears. When they couldn't sell ads, they were lifting them out of other music papers. Coupons and all.

I hinted to them that at the very least they should doctor the artwork before reprinting the ads. Days later, I came across a marked-up copy of the paper on the advertising manager's desk. A handful of ads were circled in red pencil. It dawned on me that these were the real ones. The rest were all unpaid for.

The following week, we weren't entirely surprised to be told that the paper would henceforth be fortnightly, allowing us to 'expand' to 32 pages. This meant that I had to compile two weeks' worth of billings in one go which wasn't as easy because many production folk didn't know what might be in next week's programme until they had finished making this week's!

But we battled on, and I was granted my redesigned programme pages in issue 41, published on 1 September. No longer the centre spread, and now at the same angle as the rest of the pages, they looked more like the *TV Times* layout, and I was happy with them. I also clocked the 'CGI' crudely inserted into the coupon on the back–page Coca-Cola ad!

Issue 42 – a fortnight later – was even better from my point of view. Our snapper Jack Middleton (who could be a wee bit temperamental at times to say the least) had taken some great pix for me and the rest of the paper was shaping up better. Hanley's 'DNA Man' had discovered a dark secret and although it was quite barmy I looked forward to the next episode.

But 'twas not to be. I turned up at Royal Exchange Square the

The new-look *Clydeguide* in February 1979.

The last edition of *Clydeguide* to roll off the presses.

following Monday to meet a gloomy crew. 'It's all over, Tony' sighed Roddy Forsyth, 'Jimmy's pulled the plug on us.' *Clyde Guide* had folded. 42 issues. Its last programme day was 28 September 1979. It was allowed just one year to make it or die.

As for 'DNA Man' …. I recently asked Cliff Hanley Jr how he'd escaped from having his body parts minced up by the claymore. 'Simple', said Cliff, 'he could turn himself into anything – so he turned into a midge and flew away!!'

I had waited 30 years to find that out …

How will DNA Man get out of this?

11 THE ACADEMY OF THE AIR

After *Clyde Guide* folded, I only remained with Radio Clyde for a short while as host of the weekly classical music programme, 'Nothing But The Best'. After that Karin and I set up Europe's first commercial cable radio station – which provided 12 hours a day of programmes to the new cable TV operators in the cabled parts of Scotland. The venture sadly failed, mainly on account of the unexpectedly low initial take-up of cable. But the experience of running one of Britain's very first new-style cable channels led me to the regulatory body, the Cable Authority, where I was made its first (and only) Controller of Programmes, in charge of programme standards on all of the satellite and cable channels, including Sky TV, Super Channel and MTV Europe.

From there I moved into management for a while, first as Chief Executive of Asia Vision, a cable television channel for UK viewers with roots in the Asian subcontinent. And from there it was off to Dublin as Launch Director of Programmes, planning and supervising the creation of Ireland's first satellite channel, TARA Television.

Not bad going for a Radio Clyde DJ? Don't you believe it – working for 261 almost conferred a degree in broadcasting on you! Look at the fates of others involved in the formative years of Radio Clyde ...

Two of the boys who started at the bottom as newsroom assistants – Rory McLeod and Paul Cooney – made it big. Rory climbed the ladder to the very top, selling a chain of radio stations in the south of England for serious money. Paul remained in the family for 30 years, having first moved up to sports editor and via stints at London's Capital Radio and STV reached the top of the management ladder, as managing director of the station until German owners Bauer Media passed him over for the top job of Managing Director Radio, Scotland in the spring of 2009 in favour of new man Graham Bryce. Both Rory and Paul readily acknowledge the fact that they learned about high standards and

Paul Cooney in his early days at 261.

PC teaching snooker star Ray Reardon to type!

team spirit in their early days in Anderston Cross Centre.

George Montgomery, the news reporter of a thousand voices, became Assignment Editor at Radio-Television Hong Kong. Many others from the 261 newsroom went on to greater things. Martin Frizell, a Clyde newsman from 1979–84, and the man who read the first news bulletin from the station's new purpose–built home in Clydebank, became a familiar face on GMTV.

Ben Brown, another of the newsroom team, moved on to become BBC television's Moscow Correspondent. Bill Turnbull, having spent a considerable time as the BBC's Washington Correspondent became host of BBC 1's 'Breakfast' show. Jackie Bird joined 261 at the age of 20 as Jackie Macpherson and spent three years as a reporter before becoming the main presenter of BBC Scotland's flagship television news programme 'Reporting Scotland', while over on the other channel Scottish Television's main evening news programme 'Scotland Today' was for many years presented by Viv Lumsden, one-time 'Afternoon Show' stand-in presenter, and AA traffic reporter. And Fiona Ross went from general reporting at Radio Clyde to become Scottish Television's highly respected Political Correspondent for many years.

Bill Greig returned to newspapers after his stint at 261, and George Mackintosh – another of the bulletin men – set up and became Managing Director of Radio Tay. He then joined a colleague in setting up a new and innovative telephone information service and went on to establish and run another Dundee radio station, Wave 102. Bob King moved to the information side of the Scottish Office before a spell as Head of News at Moray Firth Radio in Inverness. Marie Maguire, on the other hand, found herself changing careers to become an air hostess!

Another of the 'Saturday Boys' – the gofers who worked at weekends editing tape, filing records, writing out copyright returns – was Ross King, who after six years at Clyde established himself as a sought-after TV presenter in Hollywood.

Richard Park eventually dragged himself away from the 'Midnight Surgery', heading for London as Group Director of Programmes for Capital Radio plc before his very public role as headmaster of BBC TV's 'Fame Academy'. Voted most influential person in the music industry by Record and Radio Industry Executives in 2001, he is now Executive Director of Global Radio. Paul Coia, one of the jocks from 1976 to 1992, was the very first voice to be heard on Channel 4 Television, and is a familiar face on a range of network and satellite TV shows, as well as regular stints on Radio 2.

John Cavanagh went on to host his own programmes variously on BBC Radios 1, 2, 3, 4, 5 and Scotland.

Dougie Donnelly moved from the mid-morning show to become one of the best known BBC-TV sports presenters, not only fronting Scottish sports programmes including 'Grandstand from Scotland' and 'Sportscene', but also regularly fronting UK-wide sports programmes. Hazel Irvine, who was given a job as a Clyde production assistant when she left university, spent 18 months with the station before moving on to become another leading BBC-TV sports presenter. In 1997 she was the youngest ever host of 'Grandstand' and is regular host of the BBC's Olympic coverage.

Russell Walker and Jackie Macpherson (now Jackie Bird) in the radio car.

Steve Jones graduated through a variety of game shows on London Weekend Television and did a stint as breakfast presenter on London's talk radio station, LBC. And a young man from the North of England who came up to Glasgow to seek fame and fortune found it with Clyde before moving south as one of the main men on BBC Radio – Mark Goodier. Mark Page (or should that be Me Mark Page?) was another to have established a national reputation with the help of Glasgow's finest, going on to own a number of his own small radio stations.

On the sales side, Douglas McArthur, one-time Sales Controller at the station, moved up to be the man in charge of the Radio Advertising Bureau which looks after radio advertising sales for a whole raft of UK stations.

Andy Park continued his colourful career, first as a commissioning editor at Channel 4 Television, and then as a very successful drama producer at the BBC whose work included the ratings-topping series 'Tutti Frutti' with Robbie Coltrane and Emma Thomson. He too found himself in Dublin when he was asked to supervise the launch of Ireland's new national commercial station,

George Mackintosh.

Paul Coia.

John Cavanagh.

Radio Ireland, and he now lectures on media.

Clyde's engineering department had unimagined success. John Lumsden persuaded Jimmy Gordon that the station should diversify and start manufacturing its own studio equipment, some of which might be sold to other stations. Clyde Electronics was the result, and although it took a good few years to achieve success it was John's successor as Managing Director of Clyde Electronics, Phil Collins, who gave the company complete independence from Radio Clyde Ltd and in the process became one of the biggest suppliers of studio equipment in Europe, with Clyde designing and equipping studios in such stations as BBC Radio 1, Classic FM, Scot FM, BBC Radio Scotland, Talk Radio, Radio Telefis Eirann, Channel 3 TV Bangkok, Singapore Broadcast Company, Christian Vision Africa, and Radio Television Malaysia.

John Lumsden himself was lured to the United States by Sony Broadcast and given the job of designing radio studio equipment. From there he branched out on his own as a broadcasting consultant, now based in Texas, lucky man!

Meanwhile, John's secretary Elizabeth Partyka (known universally as 'Tyka') moved on to a star-studded career in television, rising to the dizzy heights of Managing Director at STV's programme-making arm, SMG Productions. John Temple also made it big in TV, moving on from 'The Dear Green Place' to produce 'Coronation Street' and then back to Scotland to produce the very first Gaelic soap, 'Machair', before moving on to take the 'High Road'. Bob McDowall turned his hand to record production as senior producer for Lismor Recordings, one of Scotland's major record companies.

David Murricane and his wife set up their own production and facilities company in Glasgow, Murricane & Murricane, and provide audio services for a variety of BBC and ITV programmes as well as producing many radio and TV commercials. Dave's twin brother, Paul, left the 261 newsroom for a spell as a reporter with Border TV, becoming a news and current affairs senior producer at Scottish TV before moving into public relations.

'Cuddly' Kenny Page avoided falling off Andy Park's window ledge by leaving for Israel where he was Programme Controller for the pirate station Voice of Peace before returning to Scotland as a DJ on Tay FM in Dundee. Iain Anderson was given his own daily afternoon show of classical and Scottish music on BBC Radio Scotland before taking on the station's exceedingly popular late-night show. Annie Wood went back to the BBC to run training courses for broadcasters and was responsible for nurturing many new talents who subsequently became familiar voices.

Jack McLaughlin took the decision to retire from showbusiness at the age of 40 and turned his attentions to running a successful business, dividing his time between Spain and Scotland. Colin MacDonald moved from night-time on 261 to daytime on British Forces Radio before becoming editor of a local newspaper in Glasgow, and Tom Ferrie went to host his own late-night show on BBC Radio Scotland, became Head of Music at Westsound Radio in Ayr, and then back home to Clyde 2.

Tim Stevens continues to broadcast on Clyde 2 despite a battle with multiple sclerosis, and was most deservedly awarded an MBE.

Sadly, not all our pioneers are still with us. Maggie Cockburn died from cancer at a horribly young age leaving behind a young son. George Mackintosh died in 2000. Kenny Page sadly passed away in 2002. Bob Crampsey, Don Cumming, Cliff Hanley and Frank Skerret have all left us, and jazzman turned night owl Jim Waugh died unexpectedly of a sudden and massive heart attack.

Andy Park.

Sheena Russell, whose talents as a journalist and performer had been largely wasted in the commercial traffic department, died very suddenly while only in her early sixties. Pete Shipton, our indefatigable music producer has gone, along with his wife, singer and Clyde presenter Valerie Dunbar. Colourful former boxer Freddie Mac – better known to listeners as 'Mr Superbad' – died in 2008.

Mike Russell left Clyde to become a much-loved presenter of the BBC's 'Good Morning Scotland' but eventually paid the price for his fondness for a wee Grouse, and many of his ex-colleagues gathered at his funeral to hear BBC colleague Neville Garden give a most eloquent and affectionate eulogy.

And perhaps the most successful of all the Radio Clyde alumni to have passed away, was Donald Dewar. Of course he already had a distinguished political career before he came to the station to host its Friday political programme 'Clyde Comment'. But after his spell at Anderston Cross, he returned to Westminster as an MP in 1978, became Shadow Secretary of State for Scotland and then Chief Whip. In 1987 when Labour won the election, Tony Blair made him Secretary of State for Scotland and it was he who started the process of devolution that led to the re-establishment of the Scottish Parliament in Edinburgh in 1999.

Freddie Mac aka Mr Superbad.

Donald attained the ultimate position in that new parliament of First Minister. On 10 October 2000 he died from a brain haemorrhage.

They are all missed.

Presenters – journalists – engineering – sales – management – you'd be hard pressed to find such a consistently successful combination in any other radio station in the world. Or could I possibly be just a wee bit biased?

The five of us sat anxiously in the bar of Glasgow's Lorne Hotel. Annie Wood hovered nervously at the door. Karin and I chatted to Neil Dunn, while Dave Marshall quietly sipped at a glass of beer.

It was May 5, 1997 and we were gathered together for our very first (but not the last) reunion. Some years earlier, I had bumped into Annie and we agreed to get the old gang together. Annie – always the one to look after the Clyde 'family' – contacted Andy Park, and after an interminable time we came up with a date that suited all of us. Although basically intended as a reunion of those who worked directly for Andy, many others who worked closely with the entertainment department were invited.

Slowly, in ones and twos, original members of the 261 gang appeared in the hotel doorway. Dave Marshall turned to me and whispered, 'I keep seeing people and wondering who they are and whether I'm supposed to recognise them!' I felt exactly the same. Who is this grey-haired overweight man? Oh, God, can it be … ?

'S'cuse me, I'm waitin' fur ma daughter. I can see you're waitin' fur yer friends – I'll go and sit over there.'

Phew. Not one of ours!

But as the evening progressed more and more familiar faces were greeted with whoops of recognition and affection. The jocks were all there – Steve Jones and Richard Park (who had intervened with LBC's management to get the Jones boy released from his Sunday breakfast show just for that week) – had arrived hot-foot from London. Bill Smith, Tom Ferrie, Dave Marshall, Paul Coia, Iain Anderson, Tony Meehan, Bob McDowall, and Jim Symon were all there as well. And of course our former boss, Andy Park, wreathed in smiles.

The backup team from the 'Park's Department' were there in force. Andy's original PA Eva Flannery and Evelyn MacNeil, the jocks' PA Judith Landless, record librarians Norma Beaton and

Clare Stevens, production assistants John MacCalman, Helen Clark, Julie McGarvey and Ronnie Bergman. David Meehan – who acted as agent for many of the jocks – came along, alongside the original receptionist Ruby MacGregor; Harry Barry, who spent more of his time as a musician and composer in Clyde's studios than anywhere else. Valerie Dunbar, well-known singer, and widow of music producer Pete Shipton.

From the newsroom, Paul Cooney, Karin Spalter and Paul Murricane, from the engineering department John Lumsden flew in from Florida, and was joined by his ex-PA Marion Farrell (now Mrs Iain Anderson) and former technicians Alastair Owen, Ian Couser, Jim Robertson and Dave Murricane. His now wife, one-time commercials' producer, Barbara, joined the party along with former advertising salesman Neil Dunn. Tiger Tim sent his apologies – he had a gig! And Colin MacDonald was with Forces' Radio abroad and couldn't get leave.

Bill Smith. What a swinging name!

Jonathan Dimbleby was there! He was in Glasgow to interview SNP leader Alex Salmond in a pre–general election TV programme the next day and had brought his mum to see Glasgow for the very first time in her life. The bemused pair joined us for a drink at the bar.

The evening was a giant success, with a laughter-filled meal at a neighbouring Indian restaurant whose tape of traditional Asian music was been replaced for the evening by the original 261 jingles. Everyone gave a speech, recalling scurrilous events from the past, many photographs were taken, even a quiz to tax our memories of the old days. We resolved to do it all again.

So, in 2007 we went a step further, with a full-blown reunion, this time organised by Sheila Duffy, Fiona Ross and Heather Fraser. Everybody who had been associated with the station was invited, and Jimmy – now Lord Gordon of Strathblane – addressed the troops for one last time. From technical operator Louise Tate to the infamous Charles Fitzgerald, the room was filled with more nostalgia and more of the warmth that our little family engendered.

All of this may seem rather self-indulgent, and of course it was, but it served to illustrate the extraordinary kinship that Radio Clyde created when it began. Is there any other radio or television station that could have brought so many of its original staff together again – voluntarily – for a social evening free from bitching and backbiting? Or even with! I doubt it.

18 WHAT DID WE START?

Radio Clyde was the first land-based, legally licensed commercial radio station in the United Kingdom outside London. It achieved instant success while the London stations – Capital and LBC – struggled to make ends meet. It was followed in 1974 by BRMB in Birmingham (now owned by Capital), and Piccadilly Radio in Manchester. From these humble beginnings, radio in the UK has grown to a point where there are currently a staggering 821 radio stations operating on AM, FM, DAB and the Internet.

There have been many changes and innovations, of course.

I well recall an early occasion when I was hosting the 'Popular Classics' programme on a Sunday evening, and playing a particularly quiet piece of chamber music. The IBA transmitters were unmanned, which meant that some means had to be devised for monitoring faults, etc. The boffins at the authority had come up with a fiendish device known as 'The Davies Equipment' (probably because that was the name of the company that manufactured it …) which used high-frequency signalling tones over the air to send messages back to a special control panel at the Clyde studios showing particular transmitter faults. So far, so good.

The flaw was that the system tended to detect 'loss of programme' whenever there were quiet moments. Now in the daytime there wasn't much chance of that happening since we played fairly loud music or chatter with no gaps. But in the case of the classical programme, much of the music had a wide dynamic range – which meant very quiet passages that the equipment falsely assumed were breakdowns!

The so-called high frequency signalling boiled down to a horribly loud series of bleeps which could very easily be detected by the human ear (if you're technical, they were at around 8kHz) and rather destroyed the effect of gentle music.

On this particular evening, I was damned if I was going to have my programme ruined by the weaknesses of the IBA's monitoring system. So I found a way of outwitting it.

I split the feeds to FM and AM, in such a way that the FM transmitter at Black Hill (which was monitored by other means and therefore wasn't affected by the Davies' pulses) got the normal output from Studio A, whilst 261 metres was fed from Studio C, where I increased the volume so that the Davies equipment wouldn't sense a 'fault'. Thus FM listeners heard the music in nice clean stereo, and AM listeners (who at this time of night had to contend with background interference from foreign stations anyway) had a different mix with a reduced dynamic range. All very complicated, but it worked a treat. And of course I couldn't resist telling listeners on AM that they were 'listening to radio Clyde on 261 medium wave' whilst nipping next door and telling Black Hill listeners that they were 'tuned to Radio Clyde FM on 95.1'.

As far as I know this was the very first time that any of the ILR stations attempted to 'split' their frequencies.

Although I had demonstrated that it was technically possible (indeed John had designed the studios to have such a capability from day one) the government of the day insisted that commercial radio stations had to 'simulcast' – ie transmit the same programmes on FM as they did on AM.

The reasons for this were historic. When FM broadcasting began here in 1955, few people had the new VHF receivers, and since the BBC clearly didn't want to disenfranchise the bulk of its audience, it was decided that the new VHF/FM stations would all transmit exactly the same programmes as medium wave.

Over the years, the BBC 'cheated' on this principle frequently. As well as using VHF stations to transmit special localised news and sports bulletins (in places like Orkney, Inverness and the Borders, for example) they started to put sports commentaries out on AM wavelengths while alternatives went out on FM.

Eventually, the government understood what a cruel waste of scarce frequencies 'simulcasting' was, and after dipping their toes gingerly in the water for a few experiments, they allowed commercial stations to split their AM and FM services and provide two different programmes.

Of course, not all stations initially had the resources to do so. Running two radio stations – even if both were under the same roof and utilised the same studio and technical facilities – required more people than running one, although that has changed dramatically with the advent of computerisation.

But Clyde was always one of the best-resourced stations, and on 3 January 1990, one became two with Clyde 1 on FM offering a service aimed primarily at the younger listeners, while Clyde 2 on AM (still on 261!) was aimed at more mature listeners. In addition, the night-time programming that I and others pioneered was networked from Radio Clyde's studios to commercial stations the length and breadth of the Scottish nation.

The station left its original Anderston Cross studios (Jimmy Gordon admits that at 95 pence a square yard, they were chosen on price rather than merit) and in 1984 moved to a purpose-built studio centre in Clydebank, with not only plenty of car parking space, but also a rather nice swimming pool and gymnasium.

The radio game has changed out of all recognition since Radio Clyde was first incorporated as a company on 3 February 1971.

BBC Radio has abandoned medium wave for most of its services. It has created a fifth network for news and sport. The Scottish Home Service which opted out of the London programme for but a few hours each day has given way to a fully-fledged Radio Scotland (I wonder where they got the name?) which provides round-the-clock programmes tailored to the Scottish audience. There is a full scale Gaelic-language service, Radio Nan Gaidheal, available throughout virtually all of the Gaelic-speaking parts of Scotland. There are local news bulletins for the Highlands, Aberdeen, Dumfries and Galashiels. There are also local stations in Orkney and Shetland,

How much of this would have happened, I wonder, without the competition from Radio Clyde and its sisters? In the early days, the BBC tried to pretend we didn't exist and that its commercial competitors were on the fringe of broadcasting, whilst they

The Radio Clyde team taken before coverage of a General Election. Jeff Zycinski, now Head of Radio at BBC Scotland, is second from the right. Fourth from the right, Ken Mitchell, is a BBC Television announcer-director, and Larry Sullivan (first on the left) broadcasts regularly on BBC Radio Scotland.

were at the core. It is difficult, however, to ignore a competitor who regularly turned up at industry awards ceremonies and left clutching the trophies. Current boss of BBC Radio Scotland is Jeff Zycinski. No prizes for guessing which commercial station gave him his first job in radio!

There are many challenges ahead for the commercial broadcasters and the BBC alike. The recession is having its impact on broadcasting, just as on all other forms of business. Commercial radio is first and foremost about delivering a return to shareholders, and in order to have a hope of achieving that, the industry has undergone many major changes.

The introduction – by the IBA's successor body, The Radio Authority – of national commercial stations was the first major change on the landscape. Classic FM, Talk Radio, Virgin along with Irish-based Atlantic 252 drew listeners away from both BBC and local stations. Atlantic 252 was run jointly by Irish state broadcaster RTE and RTL, parent company of Radio Luxembourg and owners of some of Europe's leading TV and radio stations. But 252 had had its day and after its transmitters were handed over briefly for a disastrous attempt at an all-sports station, the long-wave frequency was handed back to RTE for its domestic service. Talk Radio became TalkSport and Virgin became Absolute.

But through the back door came other new quasi-national networks, as smaller stations were swallowed up by big national groups and forced to take on the corporate identities of their parents. Now large swathes of the UK can tune to their own 'version' of Real Radio, Gold, Galaxy, XFM, Smooth, Magic and others.

In Scotland, the Bauer-owned 'Big City Network' (that includes Clyde 1) takes all its programmes from the Radio Clyde studios after 7pm, so those are now shared with Forth, Borders, Tay, Westsound, Northsound and Moray Firth. Likewise the AM stations in Glasgow, Edinburgh, Dundee, Ayr and Aberdeen share the same programmes for all but breakfast and a few hours at weekends.

The introduction of DAB allowed more new stations to be established in competition with the pioneers, now known in the industry as 'Heritage' stations. Although there are those in the radio business who would like us to believe that DAB is an enormous success, it has yet to gain a market share that is greater than FM. The decision to allow as many stations as possible on DAB has had consequences for the technical quality and reduced the 'bitrate' (the amount of bandwidth allocated to each channel) which means some DAB stations are in low-fi mono; not much of a selling point for a system originally intended to outshine FM never mind AM.

Efficient computerised automation has spelt the death knell for many of the original jobs in local radio. Entire stations can be run with one man and a PC. Lengthy shows can be voicetracked in a few minutes, not using razor blades and tape in the crude way I had to when faced with laryngitis, but so efficiently that listeners are quite unaware that there's nobody at the helm. When working in the USA, our daughter Julia would nip in to a local station at weekends and voicetrack for a handful of stations many hundreds of miles apart.

The internet allows practically anyone, irrespective of talent, the opportunity to create and broadcast from their own radio station. Setting aside the question of copyright payments for music played and the real possibility that some of these stations are simply broadcasting to themselves, the field is now wide open to all comers. My own internet station, *radio six international,* run purely for the fun of it and the challenges it involves, has listeners in over 160 countries worldwide and that's without any marketing! (Go on. Try www.radiosix.com)

Even conventional analogue services have undergone a revolution. When '242' was born, the Labour government argued that it made use of wavelengths that were not allocated to the UK. The powers that be stoically argued that the BBC was using all the available wavelengths. That was in 1966, when BBC radio broadcast on 13 different medium wavelengths. In spite of there being infinitely more radio stations in Europe, and therefore even more congestion on that band, the UK now uses 73 different frequencies.

Meanwhile the FM band, which, originally stretched only from 88.1 to 94.5MHz has been cleared of public utilities who used parts of it for radio-telephone services and stretches all the way from 87.5 to 108MHz meaning that many more FM stations are possible. Real Radio Scotland for example, serving the whole of the central belt, would not have been possible under the old frequency regime.

Areas qualifying for their own local commercial station have become smaller and smaller; stations serving Lanarkshire, Vale of Leven, Paisley and Renfrewshire all compete in the Clyde service area. Community radio has been introduced, with specialist stations serving both geographical communities and communities of interest. In the Radio Clyde area alone, there's Sunny Govan Radio, Insight FM (for the visually impaired community), Awaz FM for the Asian community in Glasgow, Celtic Music Radio (set up by former *Clyde Guide* man Bob McWilliam), 3TR Health Radio in Saltcoats, and Cumbernauld's Revival Radio (a Christian station); all stations with no commercial imperative and bucket-loads of innovation. True, many are run by beginners to broadcasting – but then so were most of us at the dawn of 1974.

Jimmy Gordon's original concept of small-scale radio was what he described as 'Mother Hen and chicks' with Clyde (naturally) providing a 'sustaining service' of programmes at times when the community station wasn't able to. In fact only Oban FM operates on this principle, using Clyde 2 to sustain its output.

Clyde is no longer the number one commercial station in its market. That distinction now belongs to the Guardian Media Group-owned Real Radio Scotland. Radio Clyde's endeavours begat Scottish Radio Holdings, owners of most of Scotland and Northern Ireland's commercial stations. The group is now owned by German media giants Bauer Media, for whom Scotland is just one of their many global investments.

How will all these changing factors affect Radio Clyde's future? Who is to say? None of us could have predicted the effect Clyde was to have on the topography of Scottish broadcasting when it began in 1973. But broadcasting – when all is said and done – is not about wavelengths, frequencies, digits or transmitters. It is about people. The people who listen, and the folk who broadcast.

APPENDIX 1

Wednesday, 23 January 1974

6.00am Dave Marshall • 9.00 Steve Jones • 12.00pm Richard Park • 2.00 Maggie Cockburn • 4.00 Have a Laugh with Colin MacDonald • 4.15 Ken's Korner with Ken Page • 4.30 Homeward Bound with Tony Currie • 6.30 News Special • 7.00 Citizens' Advice with Joan Mackintosh and Sheila Duffy • 8.00 The Big Bands with Ken Sykora • 9.00 Simon Moore • 10.30 Frank Skerret • 12am Doctor Dick's Midnight Surgery • 2.00 close down.

Saturday, 16 March, 1974

6.00am Rise and Shine • 9.00 Children's Choice with Dave Marshall • 11.00 Frank Skerret • 12.00pm Tom Ferrie • 2.00 Jim MacLeod • 2.30 Scoreboard with Bob Crampsey and Richard Park • 5.00 Jim MacLeod • 5.30 Pop Quiz with Peter Day • 6.00 Country and Western with Bill Black • 7.00 Hear me Talkin' • 8.00 Night Out • 10.00 Pop Party • 2.00m close down.

Summer 1974 – Weekdays

6.00am Dave Marshall • 9.00 Steve Jones • 12.00pm Richard Park • 2.00 Two at Two: Margaret Cockburn and Tom Ferrie • 4.00 Richard Park • 5.30 News Special • 5.50 Tony Currie • 7.30 Monday: Clyde's Concert Choice – Tuesday: Folk and Suchlike with Drew Moyes – Wednesday: Consumer Concern with Joan Mackintosh and Sheila Duffy – Thursday: Country Sounds with Bill Black – Friday: Clyde Comment with Tom Steele • 8.30 Monday, Wednesday: Brian Ford – Tuesday Thursday: Tim Stevens – Friday: Kenny Page with Clyde Climbers • 10.30 News • 10.35 Monday: The Anderson Folio with Iain Anderson – Tuesday: Accent on melody with Don Cumming – Wednesday: When Music was Music with Frank Skerret – Thursday: Glen Michael – Friday: The Boozie Woogie Rock Party with Steve Jones • 12.00am News • 12.05 Monday: The Folkal Point with Colin MacDonald – Tuesday: What is Pop Music? With Andy Park – Wednesday: Tom

Ferrie – Thursday: Margaret Cockburn – Friday: Boozy Woogie (cont) • 2.00 close down.

Summer 1974 – Saturdays
6.00am Tim Stevens • 9.00 Children's Choice with Dave Marshall • 11.00 Frank Skerret • 12.00 Clyde Album Countdown with Tom Ferrie • 2.00 Summer Scoreboard with Alex Dickson and Tom Steele • 6.10 The Sound of Brass with Bob Mason • 7.00 The Big Bands with Ken Sykora • 8.00 Night Out • 9.00 Hear Me Talkin' • 10.00 Pop Party • 2.00am close down.

Summer 1974 – Sundays
7.00am MacDonald's Musicbox with Colin MacDonald • 9.30 Sunday Service • 10.00 Visiting Time with Norman Ross • 10.30 News • 10.35 Personality Record Show with Jack McLaughlin • 11.30 Radio Clyde World Wide with Tony Currie • 2.00 Country Sounds (rpt) • 3.00 Folk and Suchlike (rpt) • 4.00 Radio Clyde Top 30 • 6.00 The Bill Martin Profile • 7.00 Popular Classics with Tony Currie • 8.00 Composers' Workshop • 9.00 Interact with Iain Anderson • 9.30 Jim Macleod • 10.00 McLaughlin's Ceilidh with Jack McLaughlin • 12.00am The World of Jazz with Jim Waugh • 2.00 close down.

Winter 1976/7 – Weekdays
6.00am Dave Marshall • 9.00 Steve Jones • 12.00pm Richard Park • 2.00 Tom Ferrie • 4.30 Brian Ford • 6.00 Monday: The Big Bands with Ken Sykora – Tuesday: Folk and Suchlike with Drew Moyes – Wednesday: The Sound of the Guitar with Ken Sykora – Thursday: The Sound of Brass with Bob Mason • 6.30 Friday: Clyde Comment with Donald Dewar • 7.00 Monday: Noticeboard with Fiona Ross – Tuesday: Swagbag with Sheila Duffy – Wednesday: Citizens Advice with Sheila Duffy and Joan MacIntosh – Thursday: Documentary • 7.30 Friday: So Who Disnae Like Opera? with Bill McCue • 8.00 Monday: The Aff Its Heid Show with Tim Stevens – Tuesday: The Smithsonian Institute with Bill Smith – Wednesday: Stick It In Your Ear with Brian Ford – Thursday: Clyde Climbers with Bill Smith • 8.30 Friday: The Big Bands • 9.30 Friday: New To You with Andy Park • 10.00 Late Special • 10.10 Monday: Authors with Alex Dickson – Tuesday, Wednesday, Thursday: Bookcase with Alex Dickson • 10.30 Monday: The Anderson Folio with Iain Anderson – Tuesday: Accent on Melody with Don Cumming – Wednesday: When Music was Music with

Frank Skerret – Thursday: Music Till Midnight with Glen Michael – Friday: Album Analysis with Tom Ferrie • 12.00am Monday: Folkal Point with Colin MacDonald – Tuesday: Dr Dick's Midnight Surgery with Richard Park – Wednesday: Music Round the World with Ken Sykora – Thursday: Dougie Donnelly Album Show – Friday: Boozy Woogie Rock Show • 2.00am Through the Night with Bryce Curdy.

Winter 1976/7 – Saturdays
6.00am John MacCalman • 8.00 Children's Choice with Dave Marshall • 11.00 Frank Skerret • 12.30 Absolutely Devine with Sydney Devine • 2.00 Saturday Special with Alan Taylor • 3.30 Scoreboard with Bob Crampsey & Richard Park • 6.00 McLaughlin's Ceilidh with Jack McLaughlin • 8.00 Arthur Montford • 10.00 Hear me Talkin' • 11.00 The Clyde Disco Road Show • 2.00am Saturday Night and Sunday Morning with Paul Coia.

Winter 1976/7 – Sundays
6.00am MacDonald's Musicbox with Colin MacDonald • 9.30 Sunday Service • 10.00 Talk-In Sunday with Alex Dickson • 11.00 Visiting Time with Norman Ross • 12.00 Radio Clyde Worldwide with Tom Ferrie • 2.00 Country Sounds with Bill Black • 4.00 The Other Side of Tim Stevens • 5.00 The Radio Clyde Tartan 30 with Bill Smith • 7.00 Jim MacLeod • 8.00 Clyde Classics • 9.00 Interact with Iain Anderson • 10.00 Even More Devine with Sydney Devine • 12.00am The World of Jazz with Jim Waugh • 2.00am Nightwatch with Iain Anderson.

APPENDIX 2

Technical stuff

The transmitters

Medium wave: 261 metres (1,151kHz)

Dechmont Hill (National Grid Ref: NS 647 578)
Transmitter power 2kW

In 1978 the frequency was altered very slightly to 1,152kHz
VHF: 95.1MHz Stereo (Circular Polarisation)

Black Hill (National Grid Ref: NS 828 647)
Maximum Effective Radiated Power 4kW

In 1988 the frequency was changed to 101.5MHz Stereo and the Effective Radiated Power increased to 15kW (10kW vertical + 5kW horizontal).

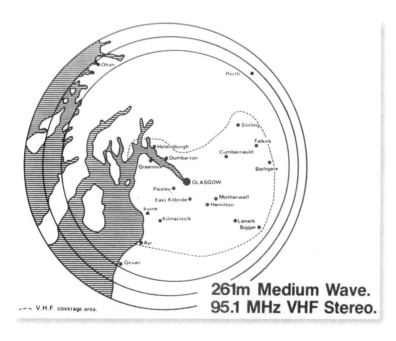

261m Medium Wave.
95.1 MHz VHF Stereo.

The Radio Clyde transmission area. The dotted area was the 'official' IBA version – the circles were the sales department's more optimistic view.

APPENDIX 3

Name that Tune!

'What's a theme tune, grandad?'

Ah, well, in the olden days each radio programme began with its own unique tune. The practice began with bandleaders in the 1920s and spread to radio shortly after.

'Oh, you mean like Neighbours and EastEnders?'

Sort of …

Here are some of the Radio Clyde theme tunes from long ago. The ones marked with an asterisk were never available on commercial discs. They were taken from pieces of 'library music' – material specially recorded for film, TV and radio use. The ones without an asterisk were released commercially and might still be around in charity shops somewhere!

Breakfast Show: 'Pretty Beaty'* – The Brandenburg 'Pop' Symphony Orchestra

Tom at Two: 'Love's Theme' – Barry White

Homeward Bound: 'Race The Sun'* – The Scottmen Plus then '7:48 Stomp' – Simon Park Orchestra

Social and Personal: 'Friendly Face'* – Peter Reno

Clyde Comment: 'New City Sound'* – Tilsley Orchestral

Radio Clyde World Wide: 'Everybody's Talkin' ' – Peter Moore Orchestra

Don Cumming: 'Bummin' Around' – Dean Martin

Frank Skerret: 'The Turntable Song' – Deanna Durbin and 'The Party's Over' – Nat 'King' Cole

Stick it in your Ear: 'Good Evening, Mr and Mrs America and All Ships at Sea' – Tom Scott and LA Express

Through the Night: 'London Hilton' – The Carnaby Street Pop Orchestra and Choir

Talk in Sunday: 'Ian Morrison Reel' – Alan Stivell

Bookcase: 'Paperback Writer' – The Beatles and 'The Day I Read a Book' – Jimmy Durante

Saturday Special: 'Portales' – The Francis Bey Tijuana Band

Scoreboard: 'Spirit of Sport'* – The Group-Forty Orchestra conducted by Laurie Johnson

The Boozy Woogie Rock Party: 'Friday Night' – Harry Barry

Popular Classics: 'Polonaise' from 'Eugene Onegin' (Tchaikowsky)

Jim MacLeod Show: 'Happy Music' – James Last Band

Doctor Dick's Midnight Surgery: 'Happy Organ' – Dave 'Baby' Cortez

McLaughlin's Ceilidh: 'Bella Fiore' – John Huband's Scottish Sound

Montford's Meeeting Place: 'They Can't Take That Away from Me' – The George Shearing Trio

Late Special: 'Contact'* – The Group 50 Orchestra conducted by Johnny Pearson.

INDEX

mcleod/gillvadin, ?G
45

MOR Record Show
es include travel, odd jobs, ch
Alex
dio Clyde's Pick of the Week's

News Bulletin (5 mins.)
Morning Show
Ken McLeo
(including the following basic components
particular order):- Where to drive today,
leisure activities for Sundays, gardening,
info. about zoos, bear gardens, etc. The
be slightly baez-ed towards religion and t

er Vew:
Joe lee
Magazine
rota basis we would handle suc
(new, old, good, bad, folk, p
he Underground Press; Poetry
ver possible. We are in conta
societies; touring groups e
Humphrey Burton

0930-1000
(-1015)

Sunday Service
Inorder to have this kind of programme from
have to admit OB difficulties and opt for a
Studio production involving two"reps." with
Reading will include occasional inserts or
material by well known guests. OB's from o
Ann and public meetings is possible and woul

Monty SPORT ?

The afternoon programme will give up-to-the-minute coverage of football, racing, etc., and the occasional irreverent look at other sports.
All this will be interspersed with bright cheery records. We are
hoping to negotiate with the S.F.A. permission to have live inserts
into our programme from any football ground. From about 1445 hrs. the
music content drops to nil, and it becomes a fairly hard sports
results programme.
1645

Needle time: 1 hour 30 minutes

Alex i/c.

Community Council
s with listener participation -
o next show.

Alex i

record show

ATURDAY
hrs. and 0700 hrs., and a 5-minute news
usic interspersed with sport, leisure, s
trips, etc., and at 0845 hrs. we schedul

45 minutes

CLIFF HANLEY
rs.: Quiz programme - format yet to be decided. *Big Prizes Alex i/c*

News including sport. *Alex i/c*

Omnibus repeat of the week's serials. *etc.*
THINGS inc Tiger TIM (AP

hrs.: Competition time. Records, and the final stages of a competition
which will have been running all week. There will be prizes (well
within the I.B.A. prescribed upper limit, I need hardly add!)

Needle time: 25 minutes

John McCalman i/c

Ben Harris pres.

AP i/c onwards

lines. A junior choice selection of
features primarily of interest to chi
of "children talking" previously tra
t this time.

ur 10 minutes

AP i/

Presenter:
0 hrs.: 2-minute news at 2000hrs. On The Town/Night Out. Outside broadcasts from two shows in our area linked from studio. The show
could also come from a restaurant with good music where we could
fade down the music for a chat with one or more dinner guests.

Needle time: Nil *Dick Park.*

t Show - Sinatra, Fitzgerald, Bas
gow humour.

5 minutes

AP i

Party. Apart from 2-minute news headlines at 2200 hrs., 2400 hrs.,
is music all the way with a heavy

leisure activities
info. about zoos, be
be slightly baez-ed

Sunday Service
Inorder to have this k
have to admit OB diffi
Studio production invol
Reading will include oc
material by well known &
Ann and public meetings

'Access' : Community Co
Local affairs with listene
overflow into next show.

News (4 mins.)
Personality record show.

Don Cunning

Big family show, records, cle
terracing, links with Canada,
of excerpt from Glen Daly/Lex
Headlines at 1200-1300, persona
football, or entertainment, int
records for half an hour.

A Park i/c   John

Old Glasgow programme -

1730 - 1800 hrs.:   Quiz programme - format yet to be decided.   *CLIFF HANLEY*   *Big Prizes*

1800 hrs.:   News including sport.   *Also i/c*

1810 hrs.:   Omnibus repeat of the week's serials. etc   *THINGS inc Trogr TIM*

1900 - 2000 hrs.:   Competition time. Records, and the final stages of a compe
                    which will have been running all week. There will be prize
                    within the I.B.A. prescribed upper limit, I need hardly add

Needle time: 25 minutes

John McCalman
Ben Harris pres.
AP i/c   forward

Presenter:
2000 - 2200 hrs.:   2-minute news at 2000hrs. On The Town/Night Out. Outsi
                    casts from two shows in our area linked from studio. Th
                    could also come from a restaurant with good music where
                    fade down the music for a chat with one or more dinner a

Needle time: Nil   *Dick Park.*

Apart from 2-minute news headlines at 2200
tes at 0200 hrs., this is music all the way w
youth appeal.

: 2 hours 20 minutes

rpie! 3d weel Arts Council 29
Woxwell
ssics *Me lee*
interviews with distinguished gues
Gibson, Yehudi Menuhin, Anthony
c. Hopefully a show based on the
sic music will begin to encourage
newer music.

Pre/ive   Presenter:
amme-repeat of part of the week
without the phone-in follow up.
conflict between educators and
rtion of this show.

CEILIDH   JA

show *late night extra*
roportion of instrumentals,
o by our own equivalent of E
andy + Clyde verger multi

Stories *roots and farem*
with synthesised music and

washed cooking
guest solo inst.

ion, whether it be musici
sts stars would be offer
ally untapped views. Po
own recording sessions

SATURDAY

Tom Hanley?

3 minute news at 0600 hrs. and 0700 hrs., and a 5-minute news at
0900 hrs. Relaxing music interspersed with sport, leisure, shopping,
what to do, motoring trips, etc., and at 0845 hrs. we schedule a
gardening spot.

Needle time: 1 hour 45 minutes

Tony Smith
Dave Marshall

2-minute news headlines. A junior choice selection of records
interspersed with features primarily of interest to children
including the best of "children talking" previously transmitted
Monday to Friday at this time.

Needle time: 1 hour 10 minutes   *AP i/c*

Skerret Show - Sinatra, Fitzgerald, Basie standards linked
humour.   *AP i/c*